THE MANAGER'S POCKET GUIDE TO

Influence with Integrity

Power, Principles, and Persuasion

Marlene Caroselli

HRD PRESS
Amherst, Massachusetts

Published by:

HRD Press
22 Amherst Road
Amherst, MA 01002
1-800-822-2801
(U.S. and Canada)
413-253-3488
413-253-3490 (fax)
www.hrdpress.com

ISBN 0-87425-522-8

Cover design by Eileen Klockars
Production services by CompuDesign
Editorial services by Suzanne Bay

Printed in Canada

TABLE OF CONTENTS

Preface

It is relatively easy to persuade others. It is *not* easy to persuade them while standing on both principle and common ground. As newborns, we influenced *without* integrity: Our cries made our own needs known, and those needs took precedence over our parents' need to sleep. We have been influencing ever since, but now we exert our influence in ways that benefit others as well as ourselves. At least we like to think we do.

In this collection of influence techniques, you will learn how to make your persuasions more powerful and more positive, thus making your sphere of influence wider and wiser. Whether you are in a position of leadership, management, sales, or customer service, or whether you simply want to learn how to exert greater influence over those you come in contact with, this array of communication tools will help you make your points more pointedly without alienating others or failing to take *their* points into consideration.

Why is it so important to add persuasion tools to your professional portfolio? Just listen to what Robert Jolles, senior sales training consultant for Xerox, has to say: "Selling is taking an idea and planting that idea in your customer's mind." So, whether you are in the loop or in sales, whether you are in management or on the shop floor, whether you are morally challenged or not—this *Pocket Guide* will give you ideas for continuous improvement of your persuasion skills, ideas for improving your interactions with customers and colleagues alike, ideas for planting ideas in the minds of movers and shakers and decision makers—all within an ethical context.

Keep in mind what Ken Blanchard has to say about the challenge for today's managers: "The key to leadership today is influence, not authority." The old days of "command and control" are gone. Thanks to the Quality movement and its emphasis on teamwork, collaborative decision-making, and empowerment, today's employee seeks to be a part of the group determining how the work is done. Persuading others sometimes means letting yourself be persuaded by the opinions about that work.

If you are reading this book, you are interested in being better than you already are. But self-improvement in general and influence improvement in particular are solo pursuits. To derive maximum benefit from this *Pocket Guide*, you will have to do some introspection. However, when insights occur in a supportive environment, they are more likely to be acted upon. That is why you will be asked to discuss some of these points with colleagues. This can be done in an informal setting between and among colleagues or in a more formal training environment.

You'll find other recommendations to engage in exercises. Again, you can pursue these informally in order to facilitate the crossover from idea to execution. You can also use the exercises in management, leadership, sales, and communication training programs.

Each tip is designed to help you explore a specific technique that will develop your influence ability. The recommendations are always made with win-win-win outcomes in mind. In other words, if you are seeking to improve your influence skills for selfish purposes only, you will not optimize the value of this book.

On the other hand, if you are seeking to improve your influence skills so that you and others with whom you are directly involved will benefit, you will find this book extremely useful. However, if you can direct your influence efforts toward three-win outcomes—you, those with whom you are in direct contact, *and* those persons or things you indirectly impact—then you will derive the greatest value of all from this book.

Note: The pronoun references are alternated chapter by chapter in order to achieve gender equity.

INTRODUCTION

IN THE BEGINNING, there was the word. Any journey that involves exploration—including the one you are on right now—ought to start with common understanding and a common language. Exemplary managers ask themselves and others, "Just what *do* we mean by the term 'customer service' or 'patient care' or all the other phrases relevant to the work so central to our lives?"

DEFINE YOUR TERMS

When we trace the origins of the word "influence," we find a heavenly connection. The ancient Romans believed that select individuals had special powers flowing into them from the gods. The assumption of strength and power and uniqueness remains to this day. To be regarded as a person of influence is to have *power*.

Unfortunately, the word "influence" can no longer be defined in simplistic terms because human interaction is getting more complicated. How, for example, can a political leader be influential on a world stage and yet not have a positive influence on children? A kind of schizophrenic or selective decision-making is foisted upon us whenever we encounter events with multiple gray shadings instead of clear, black-and-white indicators of right and wrong.

1

So, we suggest you begin this exploration by defining what *you* mean by the term "influence." Answer these questions before defining the word.

- Is the verb "influence" the same as the verb "persuade"? If so, how? If not, how do the terms differ? _____

_____

- Who is the most effective persuader you know? What specifically does he do to succeed in his persuasion efforts? _____

_____

- Think of a time when you persuaded others quite successfully. What were the circumstances? _____

_____

- Why do you want to improve your persuasion skills? _____

_____

- Recall a time when you felt more manipulated than ethically influenced. What exactly did the other person do (or fail to do) that led to this feeling? _____

_____

- In view of what you've written (and perhaps even discussed with those whose opinions you respect), how would you describe "principled persuasion"? _____

_____

_____

Having given serious thought to the definition of "influence," you can now optimize its use. Incorporate your definition into policy or mission statements; ground rules for team meetings; declarations of intentions at the start of staff meetings; and communications with internal and external customers.

Another term you may wish to define is "failure." Think about your recent attempts to influence. Surely not all of them were successful. Isolate your most recent "failure." Decide what you've learned from it, and then commit to benefitting from what you've learned. It is only by examining what we value and putting those values to work that we can be better managers.

Involve your staff in these considerations of values. Agree on and list ten values you each endorse. Then decide on collective definitions of these words. Post the definitions prominently as you interact with different departments, staffs, customers, and vendors. (You may even wish to define the ideal internal customer or the ideal persuader and then strive to develop the first and become the second.)

While you define your terms, you must also define your choices, for no matter what the moral dilemma is, you will have to consider a range of choices, from pro-activity through activity to inactivity and passivity. Take the case of Steven Jones. He was asked to certify that a gas incinerator at the Tooele Chemical Agent Disposal Facility in Utah was safe. He believed it was not, and faced this array of choices:

- To do nothing.

- To write the requested certification because someone above him asked him to do so.

- To refuse to certify, thereby delaying start-up by two years.

- To report the incident to authorities in Washington, DC.

- To quit.

3

- ■ To certify and tell himself it didn't matter that he did so.

- ■ To certify but document that he was doing it under duress.

- ■ To stall and notify the media regarding the incident.

- ■ To refuse and take the matter to his boss' boss.

- ■ To stall and contact an attorney.

As reported in *USA Today* ("Back to Work," April 4, 1999), Jones refused to certify that the incinerator was safe and was then fired for blowing the whistle. The reason cited for his dismissal, however, was "poor management skills." A federal court subsequently decided that Jones should be given his old job back.

ASSESS YOUR INFLUENCE-MESSAGE

Lawsuits like the one involving Steven Jones influence other individuals and organizations, either directly or indirectly. Virtually every action you take or don't take has an influence. In fact, you cannot *not* influence! Everything about you sends out an influence-message. The way you dress, the way you decorate (or don't decorate) your office, the kind of car you drive, the times you choose to send messages, and so on. Think about the last exchange you had during which you worked to influence others to your way of thinking. Briefly describe that exchange here.

_____

_____

_____

_____

Now answer "yes" or "no" in response to these questions.

1. I considered when my idea was likely to be received favorably _____

2. I deliberately thought about using the right tone of voice. _____

3. I chose an appropriate place suitable for the exchange. _____

4. I made certain my appearance was appropriate to the situation. _____

5. I "piggybacked" on the responses of the other person. _____

6. I deliberately chose words designed to have a positive impact. _____

7. I used body language to reflect enthusiasm, interest, and so on. _____

How did you do? If you did not answer yes to all seven questions, you might want to use these questions to fine-tune your next influence situation. When it ends, ask yourself the same questions and then compare those answers with these. Use the questions, too, as you assess how other managers influence *their* subordinates.

As you work to learn from the influence styles of others, ask yourself this—Among all the influential people you know, who has the widest range of tools in his tool kit? List those tools in prioritized fashion—the most effective one will be in first place. Then commit to using/developing one of the top four items on your list within the next few weeks.

Another way to improve your influence skills is to work with other managers (inside or outside your own organization). Begin by thinking about some job demand that is facing you. Whom will you have to influence in order to make that project successful? Gain practice before you undertake that influence discussion by working with at least three other managers who are also interested in enhancing their persuasion skills. One member of the group will serve as an observer. Here's how it works:

Engage in an influence exchange, in which you try to persuade the others to accept your idea or plan. The observer will use the questions from the preceding assessment to critique the exchange. Afterwards, analyze what worked and what didn't. Use the analysis to refine your approach before you begin the real-time, real-work exchange.

USE THE LEADERSHIP KEY TO OPEN THE DOOR OF OPPORTUNITY

Ken Blanchard regards influence as the key to leadership. You can use this key to your advantage and open the door of opportunity by using the 4-P Plan. To see just what we mean, imagine that you had a great idea this morning as you sipped your coffee and munched your bagel. Your boss walks by your desk, and you seize the opportunity to share it. "Joe," you exclaim, "got a minute? I've got this great idea I want to explore with you!"

What's wrong with this picture? Nothing, the mediocre influencer would say. After all, it shows spontaneity and enthusiasm. What boss could refuse? In truth, though, there are three potential problems with this approach.

1. Your idea needs some incubation time—time to work out the finer points, to explore the pitfalls, to gather data.

2. Your boss may not be in the mood to hear about it.

3. He may say, "Actually, I've got exactly three minutes I can spare. Get started!"

Use the Four P's to prevent these mistakes.

P #1 *Purpose*	Know exactly what you want to do and how it will benefit your boss, your organization, and your industry.
P #2 *Precedents*	Cite as many examples as you can of other successful programs that compare to your own.
P #3 *Preparation*	Explore the cost of the program (time, money, resistance) and the savings that will derive from it. Have a positive response ready for every negative point that might be raised.
P #4 *Proxemics*	Choose the best time, the best place, and the best circumstances in which to present your idea.

Managers who lead well understand the importance of time and timing. They find opportunity in those opportune moments others regard as the ordinary passage of minutes. They take advantage, too, of spare moments that others waste. When you drive home from work today, spend a few minutes thinking, instead of listening to the radio. Consider how many attempts have been made to influence you this week—at work, at home, in stores, through television, in newspapers, and so forth. Which of those attempts were successful in persuading you to do something you might not

7

otherwise have been inclined to do? Do you regret your decision? Would you let the same person/circumstances influence you to do the same thing in the future?

When you have a chance to record your thoughts, list at least three reasons for your feelings. If they were negative, vow to find ways to prevent others whom you influence from experiencing those same feelings. If those feelings were positive, capitalize on the forces that made them so.

Finally, think of specific opening lines that were used on you in recent days, lines that could be adapted to an influence situation at work. Then weigh each line in terms of possible outcomes—both positive and negative. Select the one you think has the best chance of gaining and sustaining interest in your proposal. Try it. Then log the results.

EFFECT POSITIVE CHANGE

Disraeli asserted that the secret of success is "constancy to purpose." When our energies are scattered, when we are not passionate about the idea we wish to promote or the product we wish to sell, we cannot be as effective as those who have *constancy to purpose*.

This simple experiment forces you to focus. Symbolically, it serves to direct all your energies toward the target you hope to hit. First, study the symbols beneath each number. Take as much time as you wish.

1	2	3	4	5	6	7	8	9
*	^	+	~	ø	π	°	†	£

8

Now, set a timer for three minutes. Look at the numbers that
follow. Write the correct symbol for each beneath the
number. (You may look back at the symbolse as necessary.)

8 2 7 4 9 0 2 4 6 1 5 2 6 2 7 3 0 9 5 6 7 2 6 1 7 9 6 3 1 8 7

5 0 1 9 2 8 3 5 8 2 7 8 5 2 0 7 1 2 8 5 7 3 8 0 1 9 5 2 7 6 3

Use this and similar exercises just before future persuasion
attempts. Prepare several simple "focalized-figures" exercises
like this one. Make a copy of each and exchange them with a
colleague. Then, whenever you have to influence others on
important issues, quickly develop your concentrated
constancy of purpose by doing one of the exercises just before
making your pitch. Aim each time to better your personal best
so that you can create positive change around you.

And periodically, remind yourself that without such concentration, your energies will dissipate. They will be scattered to
the winds of self-doubt, of nervousness, of trying too hard to
make a good impression. Keep the focus this exercise
demands as you communicate upwards, downwards, and
laterally.

A good example of the need to have purpose and constancy
to that purpose is found in the story of the family that drove
for several hours out of the city and into a national park for
vacation. When they opened the camper doors, the children
set about securing the camper, pitching camp, moving
supplies from the camper to the camp site, building a fire,
and so on. There was none of the usual bickering or playing

or wasting of time. The family functioned like a well-oiled piece of machinery.

One of the nearby campers viewed the spectacle with something akin to wonder. Finally, he could contain his curiosity no longer. He approached the parents and asked what their secret was.

"It's pretty simple," the father replied. "No one goes to the bathroom until camp is set up."

That same dedication will serve you well in meeting your managerial goals. Concentration exercises will help. So will answering questions, such as this one: What is the most important concept, service, or product you would like others to accept, adopt, or purchase? Determine what difference that concept, service, or product will make in the lives of those who adopt or purchase it. Then cite that difference in all your persuasion efforts. The power of the WIFM factor ("What's In It For Me?") is undeniable.

ASK THE RIGHT QUESTIONS

Management guru Peter Drucker points out that exceptional leaders know how to ask questions—the right questions. Exceptional persuaders also ask questions, of themselves and of those they attempt to influence.

Here are questions designed to hone your persuasion skills. Think of how you *typically* behave in an influence situation and answer "yes" or "no" accordingly.

1.	Do I begin by listing all the benefits?	yes	no
2.	Do I overpromise?	yes	no
3.	Do I talk more than I listen?	yes	no
4.	Do I say "I'm sorry" fairly often?	yes	no
5.	Do I dislike new experiences?	yes	no
6.	Do I believe in all my ideas equally?	yes	no
7.	Do I present ideas because it's my job to do so?	yes	no
8.	Do I dislike meeting new people?	yes	no
9.	Do I hesitate to present my ideas?	yes	no
10.	Do I dislike change?	yes	no

Although confident people will have a majority of "no" answers, the real value of this exercise lies in asking other people to assess your influence technique, using these questions to do so. Compare your answers with theirs. If you find repeated discrepancies, it's probably time to change your style.

Think of all the trivial questions asked of you each day. Then think of really significant or influential questions. Isolate the questions that showed someone was interested in your opinion. Use them (or others like them) to show your team members you are interested in their opinions.

Another way to optimize the use of questions is to prepare a list of the questions you wish specific others would ask *you*: your manager, your internal customer, your external customer, your colleagues, your staff, and so forth. (An example of a seldom asked but valuable question is this:

"What is the most important contribution you can make to the organization?") Then make another list—a list of the questions those people would probably like *you* to ask *them*. Meet periodically with those individuals and discuss the questions and answers on your list.

Try this at your next staff meeting. Ask each member to write down the answer to this question: "In terms of work, what lights your fire?" After a few minutes, ask the second question, "In terms of work, what burns you up?" Wait until they've written down their responses. Then call on each person to give his answer to the first question, while you jot down what things they really seem to enjoy doing. The next time you have project assignments to make, pull out the list and try to match talents with tasks.

Use the second question to discuss some of the areas that need improvement. Use it, too, to learn more about what tasks certain staff members dislike doing. Note: Don't call on people without giving them a few minutes to think of an answer. Otherwise, whatever the first person says is likely to be repeated by all the others.

ATTEND TO BOTH STYLE AND SUBSTANCE

It was Don Petersen, former CEO at Ford Motor Company, who declared, "Results depend on relationships." Those relationships can be grown or thrown by little things. To make them grow, keep in mind the words of Kahlil Gibran, "In the dew of little things, the heart finds its morning and is refreshed."

The way you deliver your message is just as important as the "what" of the message. Content and context are equal partners in the business of influence. The degree of receptivity you create may depend on the degree of friendliness you engender. Now is as good a time as any to assess your influence style.

You will probably not be able to complete this exercise in one sitting. Instead, you will have to reflect on the gratifying things that have happened to you over several weeks, months, and years. (It may help to think of all the restaurants, hotels, gas stations, and stores that you visit. Which stand out in your mind as being the most customer-oriented? What exactly do those places *do* to develop positive relations?) Aim for a list of 25 "little things" that have refreshed your heart, things that other people have done for you. Six possibilities have been listed to get you started.

1.	a card in the mail	13.	_____
2.	invitation to a social event	14.	_____
3.	an unexpected compliment	15.	_____
4.	a surprise gift	16.	_____
5.	a flower	17.	_____
6.	"a thank you"	18.	_____
7.	_____	19.	_____
8.	_____	20.	_____
9.	_____	21.	_____
10.	_____	22.	_____
11.	_____	23.	_____
12.	_____	24.	_____
		25.	_____

Once you have these listed your items, it's time to think about the people whom you influence or would like to influence. First, make a note of the last time you did the things on your list and the people for whom you did them. Then—to avoid duplication—lay out a schedule for using one relationship-builder each month for the various people you need to influence.

The best managers are always thinking, always on the lookout for ways to make their style and strategies even better than they are. Virtually everything you see and hear has a clue embedded in it, a clue for improving the way you manage and/or the way you persuade. For example, pick up a handful of the "junk mail" that arrives at your home or office each day. A great deal of time, money, and research have gone into the way those ads are written. Identify the little things that are employed in an effort to influence your purchase. Consider how those things could be modified to fit the influence situations you encounter at work.

REMEMBER AND DO—DO AND REMEMBER

Any persuader worth his influence-salt knows the importance of remaining undefeated by defeat. Think about the best things that have happened to you from age 16 on. Jot them down quickly on a sheet of paper. Then note how many of those events were the result of repeated attempts. If you can, isolate the specific action that finally made the walls of resistance crumble.

Good things happen to all of us, but those things seldom come from luck. Rather, they result from repeated overtures

14

to do the right thing, to obtain the right thing. In reference to your career, you will often encounter resistance to ideas or products you believe worthy of the other person's consideration. Depending on the determination of that other person not to budge, you can undertake plans that range from the simple to the complex, from the mild to the clout-dependent.

For example, if *you* cannot sway someone's opinion, possibly someone else can, preferably someone who has more clout than you do. The pilot project is another means of moving opinion closer to the viewpoint you hold. If you've met with resistance, rejection, or an outright refusal to even contemplate the proposal you are trying to make, lessen the severity of the request by reducing its scope. Ask that it be tried out for a week or two. Then, if the results are promising, ask for an even longer trial period.

You'll find, in the experiential history of your life, many successful ways to influence. Remember them. Do them. Then, once you've done them, record the process, so the next time you try to remember, you'll have recall at your fingertips. It may even help to write out a script that you can use for cold calls, hot pitches, or any situation that may cause you some stress. Dr. Murray Mittleman, an assistant professor of medicine at Harvard, recommends that we mentally rehearse stressful situations before going into them, as one way to reduce heart attack risk (*BottomLine Personal*, July 15, 1998, page 3).

ANTICIPATE CONSEQUENCES

Your next persuasion experience can be handled in your habitual fashion. Or, you can improve that fashion by considering objections you are likely to encounter ahead of time. (The Quality movement taught us that if you always do what you've always done, you'll always have what you've already got! It also taught us to believe in the concept of continuous improvement, something the most effective persuaders swear by.)

If you regard the road to successful persuasion like this:

_____

_____

then we'll ask you to consider veering off the main path to explore alternatives. If you follow this recommendation, your persuasion path might look like this:

Because the second path will lead to more interesting experiences, you will probably have more successful encounters. You will have spotted potential potholes, so to speak, and will have figured out how to get around them.

An interesting exercise that can lead to fascinating discussion is to recall outstanding historical, scientific, corporate, political, or personal failures that might have been avoided if consequences had been anticipated and dealt with. Keep a list of these, and at your next planning session cite an example or two to encourage consideration of consequences.

In one variation of the consequences theme, you draw an "If—Then" tree, using the trunk as the proposal that might be accepted. Each branch of the tree should list a "then" consequence. For example, *if* your team accepts your idea for a symposium, *then* . . . subcommittees will have to be formed, funding approved, speakers invited, and so forth. Each branch then becomes an if-stem of its own, with then-consequences listed as well. (Because the drawing will become quite extended if every eventuality is explored, use a large piece of flip chart or butcher paper.) Share the drawing with someone whose opinion matters and invite feedback before making the actual presentation of your proposal. With such preparation done before the proposal is presented, you'll have the verbal ammunition you need to overcome objections your audience might raise.

HYPE YOUR EXCELLENCE

How tactfully or unobtrusively do you hype your excellence? Principled persuaders move carefully along verbal tightropes all day long. A given idea, well-articulated, will take you to your destination at the other end of the rope. Poorly expressed, though, that rope could become the noose by which you hang yourself. It all depends on how you say what you have to say.

If you rely on your reputation, you might fail to connect with your prospective influencee. But it is possible to "brag" so unobtrusively that your listener wants to hear more.

17

Take this statement, for example: "I've been a telemarketer for the last six years. I know what I'm talking about." How could you hype your experience without sounding quite so abrasive or arrogant? Do some serious wordsmithing with the statements you typically make and refine your presentation so that hype does not sound hyper or hyperbolic.

■ How often and to what extent do you weave past accomplishments into your typical persuasion endeavors?

■ How tactfully or unobtrusively do you do this?

One technique that may help is to list ten achievements of which you are most proud. Keep the list in front of you as you attempt to persuade a colleague or staff member or even your own manager to do something you think should be done or to believe something you think will improve his life. As your share your thoughts, weave at least one achievement into the discussion as a means of illustrating your competence and lending weight to your viewpoint.

FIND EXEMPLARS

Some people consider John F. Kennedy to be the best principled persuader of the century. He managed to persuade Americans to give up the luxuries we have in this country in order to take on "the toughest job you'll ever love"—the Peace Corps. Having a good idea or a good product is not enough, however. You have to be able to persuade others to believe what you believe, to see the same vision you have in your head. (A definite contender for this title might be Kennedy's sister Eunice Shriver, whose Special Olympics have made a tremendous difference in the lives of athletes and volunteers alike.)

18

What is the power such people hold? What are the elements that constitute their remarkable persuasive excellence? Lee Iacocca believes true leaders do something unusual. "[They] tell people things they don't want to hear. It's a leader's job to get people to believe things they don't want to believe, and then to go out and do things they don't want to do." Do you know anyone who does this?

No doubt, there are people for whom you would do just about anything. How do you explain the willingness and/or loyalty you have for them? Decide how that explanation could aid you in your own influence attempts. Then use it. Extend the study of influence by asking a number of your colleagues to identify a fairly well-known figure who managed to persuade a great many others to his way of thinking. For each identified figure, determine the specific traits or behaviors that may explain why that figure was so successful as a persuader.

PREVIEW

In the next chapter we'll examine integrity, the foundation for all persuasion efforts that are principled in nature.

2 INTEGRITY

If you have integrity, others will trust you. Without that trust, it is difficult to manage people and even harder to lead them. Some of your colleagues will not give their trust until you have earned it. Others will give it more willingly, but if they ever have reason to take it back, may never give it to you again. In this chapter, we'll explore ways to influence with integrity so that you will be viewed as a person of both influence *and* integrity.

PURPOSE, BIG PICTURE, PEOPLE

Does your reputation precede you? If it is a good reputation, you want it to. If it is not, you may wind up a pauper in the realm that has trust as its coin. You will have to ask yourself some hard questions if you wish to discover how ethically you influence, how well your reputation serves you, and how much loyalty you've inspired as a manager.

Answer these questions as honestly as you can:

		true	false
1.	Generally speaking, I do what I say I will do.	____	____
2.	Generally speaking, I make sure others get the credit they deserve.	____	____
3.	Generally speaking, I listen intently to what others are saying.	____	____
4.	Generally speaking, I am trusted by others.	____	____
5.	Generally speaking, I help others grow and learn.	____	____
6.	Generally speaking, I avoid gossip.	____	____
7.	Generally speaking, I honor commitments and meet deadlines.	____	____
8.	Generally speaking, I believe a manager is there to help others, rather than to have others help him.	____	____

If you have the kind of courage that leads to self-improvement, you will want feedback from colleagues. Distribute this short questionnaire to at least ten people. Ask each person to fill it out, staple it shut, and then drop it in a box near your office. Wait until all ten forms are returned to make sure you don't know who said what. Once you know what others truly think of you, you will know in which areas you most need to improve.

There are other questions you will have to answer if you want your managerial purpose to be both an ethical and an influential one. For example,

- Why did you become a manager?

- What is the purpose behind your daily actions?

- To what extent is your staff aware of that purpose?

It may help to view purpose as a miniature version of the organizational mission, a personalized statement of how your department or your position specifically supports the larger purpose. Once that is clear in your own head, you can work to make it clear in the heads of others—internal customers, external customers, colleagues, staff members, and so on.

Purpose helps you understand how your microcosmic piece fits into the macrocosmic jigsaw puzzle. You can use this piece to influence your subordinates by:

- *Helping them understand the importance of the role they play in the organization's success.* Good managers are good communicators. They respect others as individuals and as collective members of a team organized to accomplish something.

- *Motivating them to optimize their contribution.* Study after study reveals that the average worker is not giving all he is capable of giving. As a manager, one of your most important responsibilities is to keep your own drive in high gear and to encourage others to want to do the same.

- *Offering opportunities for them to grow.* Top performers are usually motivated to take appropriate risks, to accept new challenges, to extend boundaries. In a sense, an accomplished manager is like a doctor who knows what dosages or new experiences work best, when, and for which individuals. Too much, and the employee is likely to gag on the excess; too little, and the employee will not get better. Stress the importance of the assignment you are giving as it relates to organizational goals.

■ *Criticizing with kindness.* No one likes to hear they are less than perfect. But criticism that makes us eager to pursue perfection is criticism that is well-delivered. As you work to improve the performance of your staff members, offer specific information about an event or action that worries you. Explain, too, how that behavior impacts others.

■ *Following up and through.* You've built your reputation not only on what you've promised to do, but what you've actually done after making those promises. We all need feedback, and if you are concerned about positive relationships with colleagues, you will ensure that their understanding of what will be done matches your own. If you cannot honor your pledges to them, notify them as soon as possible so alternative plans can be made.

SPHERE OF INFLUENCE

The boundaries of your influence are the boundaries of your success. Widen your sphere of influence and you'll find opportunities opening for you and for those whom you manage. The movement from the Information sphere to the Knowledge sphere has made access to information more important than possession of it.

No one knows everything, but the individual who can access anything will have infinitely more power to accomplish goals than the person with limited knowledge and no means of accessing more. This means, of course, that perfecting your

Internet skills is critical. But it also means learning who knows what and who knows whom.

If you've not already set up a knowledge base, begin today. These guidelines will help shape your initial entry into the well-connected world and will help your organization develop the "corporate memory" it needs in order to retain its past, maintain its present, and sustain its future.

1. Begin by defining the existing limits of the sphere you influence. Then branch out. Add dimension to that sphere by considering additional departments, customer sources, future employees, future events, or individuals whom you may be able to influence.

2. Regard knowledge as the bridge connecting the past, present, and future elements of that sphere. Tell significant others who will be impacted by your efforts what you are trying to do (compile a directory of knowledge-assets). Soon, they'll concur with this observation: "If we only knew what we know, we could be three times more productive than we are."

3. Begin asking some penetrating questions and recording the answers. Examples include:

   ▪ What do we know that enables other departments to do their work?

   ▪ Who needs the knowledge we have?

   ▪ How is critical knowledge preserved?

   ▪ Have the people who possess such knowledge recorded it in a uniform manner?

- How often is the information updated?

- What is the process by which people can access the information they need?

- What information do we need from other departments?

4. Do all you can to establish trust and prevent information-hoarding. To many, knowledge is power; the more knowledge they alone possess, the more powerful they feel. A good analogy might be the one given by Morrie Schwartz, subject of the book *Tuesdays with Morrie*. Waves survive, he notes, not by disintegrating when they crash against the shore but rather by realizing they are part of the ocean. If you can make your staff realize they are part of the organizational ocean, so to speak, you'll have mastered the art of persuasion.

5. Obtain visible and vocal management support. Influence those at senior levels by citing how important your plan to codify knowledge will be in the event of a disaster. Backup disks and backup plans can spell the difference between doing business close-to-usual following a crisis and not doing business at all.

6. Put critical processes on a flowchart so that when current process owners move on, their knowledge does not walk out the door with them.

7. Determine what skills are possessed and what skills are needed. Then work to fill in the gaps. We should listen to Dr. Lester Thurow of MIT: "Today, knowledge and skills now stand alone as the only source of comparative

advantage." We as managers have a specific responsibility to hone that advantage.

8. Deliberate about the informal, not-yet-recorded knowledge possessed by department members. Consider the best ways of capturing that knowledge and organizing and storing it in a repository. Commend the contributors and assure users that they will have easy access to the information in the repository.

9. In addition to the knowledge people need to get their jobs done, determine what cultural knowledge also needs to be captured. In the words of Max DePree, former CEO of Hermann Miller, corporate entropy begins to overtake an organization "when people stop telling tribal stories or cannot understand them."

   Ask around. Learn what the unspoken policies are, the unwritten rules, the attitudes and "allergies" and affinities of those at several different levels of the organization.

10. Conduct some measurement of the effectiveness of your influence efforts to enlarge the sphere of knowledge. It may be as simple as the number of hits on a database, or as significant as a major shift in corporate direction. Only by assessing can we calibrate and only by calibrating can we improve.

ROI (RETURN ON INFLUENCE)

Effective managers generally subscribe to the old saying, "Without backup data, you are just another person with an opinion." They liken the impact of influence efforts to the establishment of a knowledge base. They also assess the impact of individual efforts such as helping a given employee overcome obstacles. As employees move from dependence to independence, managers see the results of their hard work. They receive some return for the influence they have expended.

In one sense, if you have staff members who disagree with you, who question your decisions, who challenge some of your pronouncements, you are to be commended. Clearly, if they feel free to do this, then you have established a culture that respects freedom of thought and expression. (Of course, if they are rebelling against every single decision, that is a different matter.)

When your influence overtures are thwarted, don't despair. Regard the criticism as an opportunity to mutually determine the best path for the group to follow. On occasion, remind yourself of this chilling observation: *"In my entire career, nobody every questioned the morality of what I was doing."* The words belong to Adolf Eichmann, who supervised the deaths of millions during World War II. If there had been greater defiance, then a very large number of people might be alive today.

Those who complain care enough to do so. When you are faced with complete apathy or, even worse, the quiet subversion that can undermine your best intentions—then you will probably realize how healthy it is to hear different points of view or even arguments. An initially negative return on your influence is better than no return at all, because the negative contains the opportunity for conversion to a positive return. As Thomas Mann observed, "The word—even the most contradictory word—unites us. It is silence which isolates."

What will help you achieve compromise with those potentially disruptive "influences" in your department? Many managers find their persuasive powers enhanced if they are able to play many roles, rather than operate from the same behavioral basis with every eventuality. Place an "X" next to the secondary roles you feel comfortable playing in your primary role as a manager.

_____ Information-giver	_____ Surgeon
_____ Analyst	_____ Traffic cop
_____ Director	_____ Diagnoser
_____ Reporter	_____ Energizer
_____ Listener	_____ Doctor
_____ Minister	_____ Captain
_____ Coordinator	_____ Harmonizer
_____ Stress-reliever	_____ Information-seeker
_____ Teambuilder	_____ Standard-bearer
_____ Counselor	_____ Other

∎ What roles do you need to develop in order to achieve the greatest possible return on your influence? _____

_____

_____

CIRCLE OF INFLUENCE

Think of your most immediate circle of friends and family members. Consider which of those individuals have the greatest influence over you. What is the reason—beyond the fact there is love involved? Is trust a factor? Integrity? Concern for their welfare? The knowledge that they are concerned about your own? Do they influence you with their ambition? With their cleverness? With their desire to think beyond their own needs?

Whatever praiseworthy elements exist within your closest circle, they can be applied to your outer circle of subordinates, peers, and upper management, but it will require considerable thought on your part to replicate influence-driven relationships in your personal realm to those in your professional realm.

One starting point might be the process of job enrichment, which has been around for a long time. This can easily be used to deepen the professional ties that bind you to your staff members. As you engage in this process, note the elements that are operative in your inner circle of friends/family as well as your outer circle of colleagues. Strive to make comparisons.

Decide first with which staff member you would most like to have an improved relationship. Perhaps it is the one person who challenges you most often. Next, brainstorm the many ways in which his job could be changed. At this point, don't worry about whether or not the changes will work. Just contemplate them. Do the thinking at this stage without the input of the employee.

Once you have completed the list, review it. Eliminate those items that are too general or that are not possible to achieve. Review the list a second time, this time looking for changes that are simply more of the same or changes that do not add much meaning to the performance of his job. The final review should help you determine if the changes will give more responsibility, without creating the feeling that the employee is being dumped on. Is there real opportunity to learn and grow and be recognized in the changes you are proposing?

These tips will guide you in your efforts to influence others to apply their criticism toward constructive organizational improvements.

1. As you discuss the changes with your staff members make it clear that you are relinquishing some control but that you still consider yourself primarily responsible for outcomes.

2. For most of us, the opportunity to achieve is a strong motivator. Stress the inherent achievement possibilities in the changes you are proposing.

3. Point out that studies show stress is diminished as control over one's own work increases.

4. Emphasize that the changes are designed to streamline work processes—not to dump more work on the employee.

5. Allow some choice among the changes you are proposing, if only so that subordinates can select which of the changes they would like to start with.

6. Share some of your own earlier experiences in dealing with change. This will demonstrate that you have "been there" yourself in terms of growth situations. Revelations of this nature tend to establish trust between managers and their staff members.

MULTILINGUAL ADVANTAGES

The language of money

Dr. Joseph Juran notes that people at the top of an organization speak the language of *money*, while people at the lower levels speak the language of *things*. Effective managers, he asserts, should be able to converse with anyone, whether the topic is finance or widgets. If you've not yet learned what impacts the bottom line, consider taking an open-book management approach with your staff and managers. (The more support there is at the top, the more easily the approach will be accepted and adopted.)

This approach, popularized by Jack Stack, CEO of Springfield Remanufacturing Corporation, makes financial information available to every employee of the organization. Every employee knows what it costs to keep him. Sensitive data such as salary figures can be lumped together and a departmental total reported.

If you don't have a financial background yourself, find an internal or external accountant who can explain the details to your staff in an easily digestible fashion. The process will take some time, but the goal is both admirable and achievable—to help all employees comprehend the business principles on which the organization is running. When this understanding is widespread, employees will come to understand how specific actions on their part impact the bottom line.

Stack recommends starting with an income statement to illustrate cause and effect, paying particular attention to the categories that most seriously impact the organization's profits.

He also recommends making the data digestible by breaking it into bite-size pieces. Hold regular meetings, he insists, so employees can be informed and educated about the balance sheet.

The language of things

Learning to speak the language of things is often a question of finding common ground and then standing on it long enough to let the other person know you have things in common. Being able to converse in the same language requires you to listen and listen well. It requires you to ask questions about things you don't understand and to invite the other person to do the same.

The language of things is "conjugated" in both the singular and the plural. By this we mean that you will have to build upon the individual items cited by you and your staff member. When enough of these connections have been made, the two of you will be able to cross from conversations peppered with "I's" to conversations peppered with "we's."

As a supervisor, you are not expected to know the exact details of the other person's work, but you should have a general sense of how things operate. Quite literally, the word "supervisor" refers to one who has a "super" vision—that is, the supervisor has an overarching view of the way the work is done. While he may not be able to do what his staff members do (or perhaps not do it as well), he is nonetheless aware.

This awareness will lead you to greater respect for and then recognition of how your staff works. When it comes time to express your appreciation of their work, you can do it with details—so much more meaningful than gross generalizations. For example, when everyone is "wonderful," then no one truly is. Specificity suggests sincerity.

CHALLENGE YOURSELF

These are some of the skills managers are expected to possess. For each one listed, rate yourself on a scale of (low) 1 to 10 (high).

Today's date: _____

_____ Speaking

_____ Writing

_____ Interviewing

_____ Training

_____ Time management

_____ Problem solving

_____ Networking

_____ Creativity

_____ Planning/Organization

_____ **Total score**

The challenge before you is this: Take your lowest score and commit to doing something to overcome your skill deficit in this area. Your improvement efforts might mean taking a course, reading a book, reading an article, or talking to people who exemplify the skill you are working on. It may mean sitting down with your own manager to learn where he feels you need to improve. Finding the improvement path is not especially difficult. Placing your feet on it—and keeping them there—is much more demanding.

TEAMWORK

In a general sense, you, as manager, are viewed as the leader of your team of staff members. Everything you do, you do from the vantage point of a leader, even those actions you do in isolation. In a more specific sense, of course, you demonstrate your teamwork skills when you assemble your staff to advance action on common projects. Ideally, the integrity thread has been woven into the fabric of meetings and other activities that comprise the working day.

Team members and team leaders each have certain responsibilities, which can be divided into Task and Maintenance functions.

Task Functions

Task functions relate to behaviors that get the job done. For example, when you seek or give information, you are moving the project toward completion. When you summarize or monitor time, you are evincing task-oriented behaviors. When you offer alternatives or help the group to achieve consensus or assign responsibilities for the next meeting, again, you are focusing on the elements that constitute success in terms of getting the job done. But if all the team did was work on the project, social needs would not be attended to. And if friction exists among team members, they may never reach the point of caring enough to get the job done.

Maintenance Functions

If, as team leader, you brought in coffee and bagels before your team assembled, you would be displaying a Maintenance behavior. Being concerned with the physical and social needs of your staff will lead you to do such things as praising them or ensuring that each member participates. In your attempts to make certain the right amount of social "glue" is being applied, you might intervene as necessary between two disputing members; you might admonish a disruptive member or find ways to celebrate the small victories along the way to the final success.

Think of your team as a train, moving along two rails. One is labeled Task; the other is labeled Maintenance. To prevent derailment before reaching your final destination—the completion of the project—you need to move along those rails simultaneously.

Continuous Improvement

The ancients told us that the unexamined life is not worth living. In contemporary times, we have the advantage of advice from the Quality movement: "If you always do what you've always done, you'll always be what you already are." To get better, we have to behave differently. And to behave differently, we need information that tells us why we should.

One way to obtain that feedback is to periodically assess the effectiveness of the meetings you call. With this information, you can make the necessary calibrations. Without it, you will continue to do the same things over and over again. In some organizations, for example, a one-sentence feedback form is used at the end of meetings: "If you did not *have* to attend this meeting, would you have?" If the manager, functioning as team leader, receives more *yes* answers than *no* answers, and if he is interested in improvement, he will know that something will have to be done differently.

If you are not already seeking feedback, take the time now to prepare a form and distribute it periodically to your team members. You could have them evaluate the team's productivity, your leadership, or even the team's esprit de corps. Make the form efficient yet probing. And when you make changes based on what you've learned from it, let others know what you are doing. There are few actions more trust-engendering for team members than knowing what they said was taken seriously.

CREATIVITY

Creating a climate of innovation

Tom Peters asserts that imagination is the "only source of real value in the new economy." Managers who fail to see what isn't there and who have not developed a climate of innovation may be dooming and damning their own futures.

Old mindsets can easily strangle new thoughts, even before they've had an opportunity to draw their first metaphorical breath. In offices and shops and retail establishments throughout the country, employees are told every day,

"It won't work."

"It's too expensive."

"Just do your work. We don't pay you to think."

These and other killer phrases are spoken by managers who regard employees as hired hands instead of employees with hands and heads and hearts that can have tremendous impact on the bottom line.

One of the ways you can influence your staff to make those 3-H contributions (hands, heads, and hearts) is to listen to yourself. Do you ever hear yourself uttering innovation-inhibiting statements that cause thought processes to freeze up and employees to *shut* up? If so, you are effecting a lose/lose/lose situation: You lose because your leadership is diminished. The employee loses because he feels unappreciated. And the organization loses because the employee will stop making suggestions. In such cases, the loss to the organization is impossible to estimate.

Encourage your staff members to fight for their creative ideas. Remind them often of people like:

- *Guiseppe Verdi*, who was declared "insufficiently talented" by members of the Milan Conservatory.

- *Walt Disney*, who as a child was told he had no talent.

- *Albert Einstein*, who was called before a headmaster who told him, "Your mere presence offends me."

- *Grandma Moses*, who was told she was too old to start painting.

- *Wilma Glodean Rudolph*, who, doctors predicted, would never walk again after being stricken with polio during childhood. She didn't walk—she ran—all the way to an Olympic gold medal.

Encourage your staff to take rejection in stride and to consider alternatives if their first ideas are not accepted by you, by the team, and/or by upper management.

Techniques for engendering creative thought

■ *Janusian Thinking*—Janus was the Roman god whose face appeared on ancient coins with two profiles showing. He looked back over the year that had just ended and looked forward at the same time to the year about to begin. (The month of January is named for him.) Janusian thinkers are able to hold two extreme perspectives in their minds at the same time. They ask questions such as,

- ■ "Does bacon have to come in strips?"

- ■ "Do puzzles have to be on a flat surface?"

- ■ "Do mystery-story readers have to wait to the end before the murdered is revealed?"

This kind of thinking has led to creations such as round bacon, three-dimensional puzzles, and a detective named Columbo. It has also led to interesting possibilities such as winter golf, housing senior citizens on college campuses, and living funerals.

■ *Juxtaposed Disconnects*—Using this technique, take a series of paired words and use them in relation to a problem the team is facing or a decision that has to be made. Some combination might be:

birdseed/scissors; power/ice; pharmacy/squirrel; field/telecommuting; eyeglasses/vein; resume/sleeve; prediction/summit; pressure/appeal; focus/ilk; modem/vitality; skin/candy; book/bunion; money/grape; brick/curl; car/fox; port/thread/; rainbow/caterpillar; clock/phobia

The trick is to take a question such as "How can we increase the number of suggestions submitted by employees?" and explore the possibilities via an unusual verbal combination, such as "umbrella/chord." Thinking along these lines might lead to ideas like the following.

- Umbrellas protect us from inclement weather, and good ideas can protect us from inclement financial weather by showing how the organization can save money, create jobs, or outstrip the competition.

- An umbrella has many spokes, and a good suggestion system needs a climate for innovation, support from upper management, recognition on many levels, and a communication system that provides feedback.

- A chord is composed of many different notes. Perhaps team suggestions should be encouraged, along with team rewards.

- Chords can sometimes sound discordant. Perhaps those ideas that we are tempted to label "impossible"—because they are not in harmony with the existing way of doing things—should be shelved until a later time.

■ *Big-Picture Thinking*—The story of the society matron who held a formal dinner party in her elegant home provides a good example of how the mind works when it moves beyond the immediate focus. Seated at her table was a rather boorish guest who, at one point, speared the meat on his plate and held it up to her. "Is this pig?" he demanded to know.

Most of us would have answered yes or no. But this woman moved the question beyond the literal and into a higher sphere. "To which end of the fork are you referring?" she asked in the politest of tones.

When we are able to transcend the narrow elements of the here-and-now and elevate our thinking to a different place, a different time, an even bigger issue, then we are engaging in Big-Picture Thinking. One thing that helps is to take time to list all the available resources that can be used to solve the problem. We so often overlook this important source of assistance. A second list should be created as well: the names of individuals whom we are not certain can or will help but whom we intend to ask so we'll know if we can place them on the first list.

Garnering support for your ideas and for your team's ideas

It's not enough to have good ideas. In order to turn those ideas into organizational realities, you need to persuade others that the ideas deserve the time, money, and energy required for implementation. You can win funds and influence people by practicing some or all of the techniques that follow.

■ *Anticipating*—Like a well-rehearsed trial attorney facing a jury or a skilled president facing the press corps, influential managers have anticipated reactions and the decision makers likely to have those reactions. But you have to go beyond realizing what is likely to happen when you make your proposal and actually fashion the response you would give to the reactions you foresee.

■ *Paraphrasing*—There will be times when you hear something that sounds like an attack on your proposal. And it very well may be an attack. But it may also be a simple question or a request for clarification. Learn to frame the

41

question or comment in a more positive light as you repeat it for the others to hear or think about. Here's an example. During your presentation, one member of the approval-granting body remarks, "If we do this, we'll be going so far out on a limb that we're likely to topple into oblivion."

You want to capture the essence of the person's comment without adding to the negativity it contains. You might paraphrase like this: "Warren is wondering about the risk factor in this proposal. It's not as risky as it seems. The very worst that could happen is that the focus group submits a negative report. We don't need to go public with that. Granted, some members of that group might talk about the experience afterwards, but it's unlikely they would hold a press conference or write an editorial. They might tell their friends and families about the open-forum sessions, but even then, it's a limited number of people who would know what went on at the meetings. And let's keep in mind that unless we get this feedback—both positive and negative—we won't know how the public truly perceives this new venture of ours."

▪ *Converting comments to questions*—A variation on the paraphrase theme is to offer a mild challenge by asking a question in response to a statement made by someone in your audience. If you are met with a bald declaration like, "We tried this four years ago and it failed," you might ask, "Did it really fail? Or was it put on hold because Susan was transferred to Europe before she could launch it?"

▪ *Citing a higher authority*—Successful persuaders—like professionals in every industry—have their own tricks of the trade. One of those is citing a higher authority. So if you

42

remember the CEO of your firm had written a letter several months ago urging employees to think outside the box, and if you are being criticized for a proposal that is somewhat unorthodox, you could refer to that letter for indirect support. Few people would dare contradict a dictum that originates in the highest circles. Even if you do not have access to the viewpoints of the upper echelon, you could cite other individuals who do share that viewpoint and are generally widely admired.

▪ *Going out on a verbal limb*—Within the animal kingdom, the survivors have acquired a range of requisite behaviors. They have learned to adapt themselves to different threats in order to stay alive. By extension, you'd probably agree that different folks need different strokes. But have you managed to alter your language or alter your approach, depending on the personalities of key decision makers?

If so, you probably know that some prefer a lighthearted rather than a heavyhanded method. With such a person, you could go out on a verbal limb as a way to ensure receptivity for your idea. For example, "Joe, I am so convinced this is going to work that if it doesn't, I'll wear a tee-shirt labeled Dunce for one entire month." (In a worst-case outcome, keep your word!)

▪ *Asking what constitutes satisfaction*—You've made your proposal. Now you are fielding questions about it, some of which have an adversarial ring to them. Instead of becoming defensive, try turning the tables. Ask the relentless naysayer any of these questions, "What would you like me to say?" "What would lead you to declare this a workable option?"

"What would you do if you were in my shoes?" "What would satisfy you?"

▪ *Citing precedents*—No matter how good you are, no matter how good your idea is, it needs all the support you can gather. An excellent source of support is the past. If there are precedents for the concept you are proposing—either in your own organization or in related industries—cite them. If you can, you can profit from having half the battle already fought by others who were successful in overcoming opposition. Their proven track record can be employed by you as you work to influence others to adopt your idea.

R-E-S-P-E-C-T

Recognize

Hubert Humphrey once noted that the true test of a society is how it treats the least powerful members of that society. In a similar vein, the true test of a manager may well be how he treats the least powerful members of his staff, of his organization, of his customer base. The superstars have been "accoladed" often. In fact, their own drive for achievement is probably their greatest source of satisfaction—not the recognition they receive from colleagues. But the newer staff members, or those who work behind the scenes, or those who are seldom noticed—these are often the individuals most deserving of recognition.

Keep a simple log noting when, where, and how you gave recognition to various individuals. Vow to make such recognition equally distributed in nonequal ways. In other words, if someone has done an especially good job on a project, you might take him to dinner. If someone else succeeds in landing a big account, recognize him in a different, but equally meaningful way. You might even consider asking staff members what their preferences are before you recognize them.

Encourage

One of your many responsibilities is to encourage staff to develop their potential. A model that may help is the A-C-T-I-O-N Approach, which helps you and your staff members determine the gap that exists between actual performance and desired performance. Once that gap has been identified and analyzed, then a corrective strategy can be devised.

A - **Ability**

Determine what the employee knows how to do well and what the employee should know. Reach agreement on the gaps and the extent of them. Then arrange for training to narrow the gaps. Don't limit yourself to the formalized concept of training. It may be the employee will learn best by "shadowing" a more experienced employee for a day or by reading a book or article, listening to an audiotape or gaining some hands-on experience. Agree on a plan of action to close the gap.

C - **Conferences**

It is not enough to meet at the beginning of the A-C-T-I-O-N process and then at the end. Your conferences with the individual must become a regular part of your relationship. In this way, you will both have the feedback necessary for the Plan-Do-Study-Act cycle that is integral to successful implementation.

T -   Time frame

Time plays a key role in making the A-C-T-I-O-N
Approach work. What is the time frame you and your
employee have established for this plan? Consider not
only how long it will be in effect but also how often
you will meet to see that milestones and deadlines are
being met as scheduled. Consider, too, how you will
measure improvement and—if it is not happening—
what additional time can be committed until it does.

I -   Incentives

Management expert Michael LeBoeuf insists that
what gets rewarded gets repeated. In fact, he claims
this is the only thing managers have to remember if
they are trying to improve productivity. What
incentives will you offer your employee as he works
to narrow the gap by improving the way he does his
work? Believe it or not, money is not the only or most
important motivator for the average employee. Being
included in meetings, for some, is a validation of their
worth. For others, it might mean having you ask their
opinion. For still others, the incentive may be the satisfaction that comes from knowing they are growing
in their professional stature or making themselves
more marketable. And, of course, for some it will be a
raise. Learn early on what the employee would like
the outcome of this A-C-T-I-O-N plan to be and then
commit to some reward he will find satisfying.

O -   Optimization

You may be surprised at the answers you'll get to this
question: "What prevents you from being even more

productive than you are?" Or to this one: "If you could do the work the way you think it should be done, what would you change?" Often, we are blocking optimization of employee efforts without even realizing how much of a blockade we are. Encourage an honest and open exchange of ideas about ways to work smarter.

N - Necessities

It's fairly easy to complain, and many employees revel in doing just that. It's a bit more challenging to do something to eliminate the cause of the complaint. Your people skills will be called into play as you seek to learn what things your staff members need. Encourage direct comments to you, rather than gripes behind your back. Explain that you are not a mindreader and you can't solve a problem if you don't know it exists. Identify needs not only at the beginning of this plan but at various stages during its implementation, too.

Stretch

There is magic in thinking big. Ideally, you've experienced it by this stage in your career and can help others do the same. Acknowledge that the impossible is often the untried and then begin working with your staff to stretch their ways of thinking. Here are some tips that will help.

1. Brainstorm ways to make improvements.

2. Make a flowchart of the processes of the department as a whole and the processes of individual staff members. This means starting with an "input," which is what gets a work process started. Go immediately to the "output," or the action that

signifies that particular process has ended. Next, list each step in the process by using rectangles and arrows leading to the next rectangle-step. When you reach a decision point, write it in the form of a question that can be answered by "yes" or "no." If yes, trace what actions will be taken. If no, trace those steps instead.

Ask a lot of questions once the processes are flowcharted. For example, if one step of an existing process is to send a requisition to the manager for approval, ask if such a step is really necessary. It may help, too, to draw another flowchart, one that shows the ideal way of doing the work. Then compare it to the actual flowchart and look for ways to streamline.

3. Benchmark. Learn what other organizations are doing and see what modifications can be made for your own circumstances. For example, the State of Michigan holds a "Six Weeks to Wellness" program each year. Every state employee is given information about physical and mental good health and is encouraged to follow the steps to improved health during a six-week period. Could your organization do something similar? Probably. It need not be a wellness program, of course. There are innumerable ideas out there, but if you don't stretch yourself to find them, they'll remain in the unknown, and thus undone, realm.

Jack Welch of General Electric said this: "If the rate of change outside the organization is greater than the rate of change inside the organization, then we are looking at the beginning of the end." And, the U.S. Office of Personnel Management lists "vision" and "external awareness" as the highest competencies in a list of requisite management skills. Become aware of what is happening in the outside world and then take steps to make sure your own organization is prepared for the eventualities bound to occur.

Please

Childhood chants are often relevant to the workplace. Remember "All work and no play makes Jack a dull boy"?

There is some relevance in the statement as far as managers are concerned. What are you doing to make the environment a pleasant one? What steps can you take to reduce some of the stress employees are experiencing? Is your manner an abrupt one? It takes some serious introspection to determine what you can do to make the workplace a more pleasing place to be. These examples may inspire you.

■ At Ben and Jerry's Ice Cream factory, "Joy" clubs meet periodically to determine ways to bring joy to the workplace.

■ At Datatec in Fairfield, New Jersey, customer surveys are conducted via in-store computers. The employee with the highest score at the end of each quarter receives a plaque. His or her spouse receives a letter of appreciation and a dinner-for-two certificate.

■ The CEO of San Francisco's Concept Kitchen has hired a masseuse to give massage therapy to staff members every other week.

■ Managers at Strategy Associates in Foster City, California, are expected to reward their teams by having them leave early or go to the beach or go take golf lessons if they've done an especially good job on a project.

Your efforts to please your work staff need not be expensive —just creative.

Exact

Thanks in large measure to the Quality movement, phrases such as "good enough for government" have been replaced with phrases like this one from Lexus: "The relentless pursuit of perfection," or the statistical precision in the term "Six

Sigma" or the idea of "zero defects" or the phrase, "When good enough isn't."

You'll not reach an improved level of efficiency or customer satisfaction or accuracy or cycle time unless you are doing some measuring. Involve your staff, your customers, your own manager in determining what most needs to be fixed in terms of the outputs of your department. Then collect baseline data to learn what the existing conditions are.

Inspire your team to develop an action plan that will improve those data over a specified period of time. Then, re-measure to learn if improvement actually did occur. If so, continue with the action plan. If not, develop a new one and measure again after it has been fully implemented.

Cohere

Archaeologists have uncovered ancient maps that designated unknown regions with some very interesting labels. Sometimes the unexplored areas were called "terra incognita," Latin for "unknown land." Other labels included the words "There be dragons," and "More beyond." The future, of course, is an unexplored territory, one with dragons of a different kind. As a manager, your task is to create bonding that will inspire your staff to anticipate what lies beyond, rather than be paralyzed by the prospects of the future.

You can influence that bonding by:

1. Engaging in occasional and random "positively outrageous service," a term coined by author T. Scott Gross. Even if you only do this once a year, plan some unannounced, unexpected,

unheard-of way to develop esprit among your corps. You might, for example, hold your annual Christmas party smack-dab in the middle of July. Or assemble the staff to watch a half-hour video on stress reduction, such as those that feature comedienne Loretta LaRoche.

Your staff, in a sense, are your customers, for they receive from you what they need to start their work processes. When you "supply" them with these inputs, you are the supplier and they are the customers. As such, you owe them the best possible service—not only in the work-relevant sense but in the psychological sense as well.

2. Celebrate the typical and the nontypical as well: Make certain that every staff member is honored at least once during the year, and that no staff member is honored excessively. Typical celebrations, of course, are birthdays or work-anniversary dates or engagements. But learn about your staff members so that a celebration can be held if someone's son won a scholarship or someone's wife received a promotion in a different company. It makes everyone feel good to work and celebrate together.

Listen to what Harvey Mackay, CEO of Mackay Envelope Corporation and author of two business best-sellers, does. He has a 66-question profile that salespeople have to complete on each of their clients. "You wouldn't believe how much we know about our customers," he brags. You can modify the approach, of course: Choose 22 questions or 5 or 10—and use them with your staff. The knowledge can be applied in numerous ways.

One example from Mackay involves a child: "We had the entire Minnesota North Stars hockey team autograph a goalie stick for the son of one of my buyers, the goalie on his junior high school team, hospitalized with 12 stitches and the outline of a puck on his forehead" (*Successful Meetings*, "Route 66," June 1992, page 28).

3. Involve the staff in some project that goes beyond them to reach out to the less fortunate. Try spending one weekend a year building a Habitat for Humanity. Or appoint one person to be the collector of loose change. Once a week, that person collects small coins from all his colleagues. If the donations total a mere $5.00 a week, your staff can sponsor a child living in impoverished conditions in a foreign country. The Save-the-Children Foundation is but one that will arrange for you to make a big change in a little person's life. The funds go toward community development, helping families to help themselves. Your staff can correspond with the child and will receive an annual progress report on community-development activities.

Author Joyce Lain Kennedy maintains that motivating people to contribute their time or expertise is what leadership is all about. And millions of volunteers will tell you: one of the very best ways to feel good is to do good.

Teach

If you read about the character traits of successful individuals, you find the same elements repeated over and over. Teach your staff members new and effective ways to acquire and/or develop these qualities. Several are listed here.

Optimism   What are the tips, tricks, and techniques with which you keep yourself motivated?

How can you share those with your staff as a whole and with individual members? Some managers swear by the self-talk process; they engage in an internal dialogue and use it to assure themselves that whatever hurdle they are facing is surmountable. Others remind themselves of their personal heroes, people who overcame huge odds to emerge victorious. Still others hang motivational posters in their office or recollect past successes to get into the "go-get-'em" frame of mind.

You've doubtably taught yourself some techniques over the years. Model those indirectly and share them, more directly, with staff.

Opportunity   Even in the most dire circumstances are the seeds of opportunity. In fact, the Chinese calligraphic symbol for "danger" is joined with the symbol for "opportunity." You've heard the truisms—"Every cloud has a silver lining," "It's always darkest before the dawn," "The deeper sorrow carves into your being, the more joy it can contain." Acting on those beliefs, though, is what leadership is all about.

Network   To paraphrase a popular song, "People who need people are the pluckiest people of all." It takes a little bit of courage to network—after all, you are essentially reaching out to strangers and asking for their help. But the benefits to you, your team, your organization, and even to the individuals with whom you network are innumerable. Some organizations have even appointed Chief Knowledge Officers, whose job is to develop formal intellectual networks by tapping into the informal personal networks that exist in every organization.

Demonstrate your pluck, in a microcosmic way, by determining who knows what and who knows whom that will make the operation of your department smoother, faster, or less expensive. Learn what is being done in the firms where your staff's spouses, sisters, friends, and neighbors work. Someone out there has solved the very same problems you are now facing. Ask your staff to engage in networking as a way to increase the department's productivity.

Open-mindedness As ironic as it may be, your strengths can actually become weaknesses if you rely on them so often and so completely that you don't leave yourself open to new possibilities. Periodically, encourage open-minded thinking by illustrating, in the gentlest way possible, that no one has all the answers. For the next month, try starting staff meetings with a question that everyone thinks they have the answer for. To illustrate, "How long did the first U.S. satellite stay in space?"

Have each member offer an answer and then share the surprising truth: The first U.S. satellite was actually in space for twelve years, from 1958 to 1970. Such startling information is usually a sufficient eye-opener. As solid and secure as we are in the knowledge we need to perform our jobs well, we may be operating on some incorrect assumptions. Or the knowledge that has served so well so far may be shifting, making new knowledge more valuable.

Another way to influence staff to be more open-minded is to share advances being made in your industry. Learn what is happening in the outside world that should also be happening in the inside world, where your staff spends half of its waking hours each workday.

Energy People with energy energize others. Think about leaders you've known or known about. Imagine them in your mind's eye. Chances are, you are seeing some whose vitality transcends circumstances, whose enthusiasm is readily apparent. This energy seems to ignite sparks in others, catching them up in comparable waves of willingness and interest. When you feel passionate about a topic, you derive energy from that passion.

Of course, people who are in good physical shape have another kind of energy. Think about ways to influence your staff—without sounding preachy—to take better care of themselves. Wellness programs abound, as do programs to reduce stress or resolve conflict. Think of what your team could accomplish with all the extra energy that can be generated when such programs are at work.

Risk-Taking Going out on a professional limb is good for all of us once in a while. Influence your staff to take appropriate risks by establishing a climate in which mistakes are tolerated but repeated mistakes are not. If you need a mistakes advocate, use Bill Gates, who says, "It's fine to celebrate success, but it is more important to heed the lessons of failure. How a company deals with mistakes suggests how well it will bring out the best ideas and talents of its people and how effectively it will respond to change" (*USAir Magazine*, "Bill Gates: The Importance of Making Mistakes," July 1995, page 48).

Make your tolerances known to your staff and offer them guidelines for their "risky" ventures. For example, you want to be informed of expenditures that cost over $1,000. Or you want progress reports every two weeks. Or if customers will be contacted directly, you'd like a copy of the letter that would be sent. Such safeguards will not prevent all backfires, but they'll catch quite a few. For those missteps no one foresaw, take them in stride but do all you collectively can to make sure they don't happen again. And keep a file titled "Lessons Learned." Ask teams to review its contents each time they undertake a new project.

PREVIEW

We'll take a look in Chapter 3 at the kind of statements that de-motivate as well as the kind of statements leaders use to influence. Also discussed are ways to overcome objections and how to make your writing more influential. The chapter concludes with techniques to make your words more memorable.

3 ◆ LEADERSHIP

Leadership and language are lifelong companions on the journey labeled "professional success." You may have good ideas for saving money or cutting costs or increasing productivity. But these ideas will not sell themselves. Your ability to persuade others, to ignite them with the fire that is in your belly, may spell the difference between the birth and death of your proposals. The former head of the American Management Association, James Hayes, once remarked, "Leaders who are inarticulate make us all uneasy." And when we feel uneasy, we are not inclined to follow our leaders.

NONINFLUENTIAL STATEMENTS

Civility

Many thought-leaders in the country today bemoan the loss of civility. Others, such as Tom Peters, are taking pro-active steps on its behalf. Says the *Excellence* author, "I devoutly believe that little touches matter. . . . In fact, I've spent much of the last decade and a half trying to get busy plumbers, physicians, and semiconductor-makers to pay as much attention to these very human actions as to grand strategy" ("Free Markets, Bumpy Rides and Necessary Sacrifice," *Office Systems*96, March, page 66). The little touches to which he refers are thank-you notes.

If we influence with civility, then it follows we will not be influential with incivility. In fact, a front-page story in the business section of *USA Today* tells of a woman who received a check for nearly a half-million dollars by mistake. ("$473,130 goof raises pension-control concerns," by Elliot Blair Smith, March 29, 1999). She returned the money but was never acknowledged for having done so. An angry relative called to demand she be thanked. The story made it to the office of the chairman of the Senate Committee on Small Business (who deemed it an outrage) and then made it to the pages of several newspapers as well.

Incivility, according to research done by Christine Pearson at the University of North Carolina at Chapel Hill, reveals that of the 775 respondents who have experienced an unpleasant interaction at work, 12 percent intentionally decreased the quality of their work; 22 percent decreased their work effort; 28 percent said they lost work time trying to avoid the other person; 52 percent said they lost time worrying; and 46 percent contemplated changing jobs ("Incivility costs firms money," *Democrat & Chronicle*, June 8, 1998, page 5F).

You are not exerting a positive influence on your subordinates if you fail to express appreciation. Worse, you may be negatively impacting the bottom-line if your communications are abrupt or abrasive. Look for these signs that your management style may be destroying initiative:

	Yes	No

■ *Does your staff hesitate to tell you the bad news?* ____ ____
If they do, it may mean they fear you'll "shoot
the messenger" or that you don't tolerate
mistakes.

■ *Is there evidence of groupthink?* ____ ____
If so, it may mean your employees are afraid to
challenge you.

■ *Do you get full agreement on every issue?* ____ ____
If so, it may mean your staff is trying too
hard to please you. (Tom Peters tells people,
"If you have gone a full week without being
disobedient, you are doing yourself and your
organization a disservice.")

■ *Do you hear truly unusual ideas presented
at staff meetings?* ____ ____
If not, it may mean you have not created a
climate for innovation. (Remember, Peters
also asserts that "every organization
should have at least one weirdo on staff.")

■ *Do staff members appear awkward in
your presence?* ____ ____
If so, you may be sending out messages
(deliberately or inadvertently) that "all work
and no play" is the function of your
department.

■ *Do people joke around with one another?* ____ ____
If not, it may be that the culture is so grim and
the morale so low, productivity is
imperiled.

Of course, the lack of civility may be coming from other sources. In this case, you have an obligation to protect your staff from harassment of any and all kinds.

Open mouth; Insert foot

If the bold statement above describes something you do at least once a month, now is the time to make some changes in your verbal strategy. You've probably heard the unending criticism of IBM Chairman and Chief Executive Office Louis Gerstner, who said at a press conference, "The last thing IBM needs right now is a vision."

While it's true that from time to time everyone says something she regrets, you can nonetheless train yourself to think before you speak. One thing that will help is to have confidence in your brain power: the average brain operates at a speed of 800 ideas, words, thoughts, impressions, images a minute. This means you can internally see or hear the danger long before the words come tumbling out of your mouth. Be sensitive to the red flags that begin to rise when you are on a dangerous verbal road. They will warn you in sufficient time for you to get off that road and on to another.

Better still, do assessments of the circumstances at all times and avoid any topics that might make others feel uncomfortable. Make it a point to learn which words are offensive to which people. A phrase like "just a" in front of the word "secretary" may sound acceptable to you, but it is bound to alienate more secretaries than merely your own. "The final solution" may sound like a workable problem-solving tool to you, but if you use it as the title of a column, as a leading magazine recently did, you will probably find yourself

60

offering apologies for the sinister, Hitler-like connotations of the phrase. The magazine did.

Insensitive comments can not only cause great harm to others, they can be dangerous to the health of your career. Texas Judge James Barr, for example, lost his job after a number of indiscretions, among them his description of a three-woman prosecution team as his "all-babe court."

Learn how much gold there really is in silence. The things you don't say will never cause as much trouble as the things you do. At the very least, pause to collect your thoughts. And know that you can refuse to comment. Washington reporters, with begrudging respect, have noted that presidents have a dozen ways to say "no comment."

Of course, when you are engaged in "upward" communication, avoid phrases that put you in a bad light. For example, if you are prone to explaining a stalemate in work progress by saying, "I'm waiting for so-and-so to get back to me," you are, in effect, suggesting that control of the situation belongs in the hands of other people rather than in your own.

If you preface your comments by saying, "This is probably a stupid question, but . . . ," you are signifying a lack of confidence in yourself. Worse yet, you are prejudicing others to view your comments unfavorably.

If you use the phrase "I've been so busy" to explain why you haven't returned a call, you are providing an excuse that most people will find unacceptable. *Everyone's* busy, but other people manage to make the calls they have to make within an acceptable time frame. It's better to say, "I've been working all week on our budget projects and I finally had a chance to get back to you today." "So busy" has an empty ring to it.

And, of course, listen to yourself. Phrases that you say all too often become tired and meaningless after a while. There are a million words in our language. Find some new ones to express your thoughts.

HOW LEADERS USE LANGUAGE TO INFLUENCE

The effective manager has two hats in her closet: one labeled "managing" and the other labeled "leading." Sometimes you wear the hat that makes sure everything is running smoothly and that the status quo is being maintained. At other times, you deliberately upset the status quo by making a positive change. In both cases, you need the support of colleagues, and it is primarily through your words that you will influence them to join you in either continuing the status quo or upsetting it.

Your actions, of course, reflect your attitudes as well as your ability to manage and to lead. But your words reveal just as much, perhaps even more, about your attitude and ability. The way you handle everyday challenges or once-a-year crises, for example, can either demoralize your staff or inspire them to greater achievement.

Defusing timebombs

Do you thrive on conflict or recoil from it? Ideally, you chose the first option, because no manager's life is free from conflict—if only the battle to stretch limited resources. Even if you are winning the battle, it can fray tempers and leave your staff edgy. Here are suggestions for keeping your temper in check so you can defuse timebombs instead of igniting them.

1. Anticipate what can go wrong and be ready for possible eventualities. You might, for example, don your leadership hat in staff meetings by asking:

- What can go wrong?

- What have we forgotten about?

- What is crippling other departments?

- Are we ready for _____?

- Whom do we need to talk to?

- What's happening in the outside world?

- What might prevent us from meeting our deadline?

Translate the worries that keep you up at night into well-worded incentives to motivate your staff toward preparedness. Assigning small projects to different staff members will give them the self-confidence they need to develop their own leadership potential. For example, if you live in states where the earth occasionally rumbles, you could assign one person to make sure each office has an emergency preparedness kit. Another person could learn what has to be done before a blackout or a worse-case scenario like the bombing in Oklahoma City occurs.

2. The timebombs might also be contained within your staff. If you suspect someone has deep-seated psychological problems, you owe it to all concerned to get professional help

for that individual. If, on the other hand, the timebombs are merely the occasional flare-ups that occur naturally in families and workplaces alike, you can do much to soothe ruffled feathers. You can hold conflict resolution training for the entire staff or show a video on the topic in lieu of a staff meeting one week. You can meet with the individual(s) who does not seem to be holding up well under pressure and offer advice gleaned from books, magazines, and other managers. You can develop esprit de corps by involving the whole staff in nonwork-related events. And if two staff members are warring, you can serve as the mediator until their conflict is worked out.

3. Serve as an exemplar for your staff. For example, if you come under attack from them or in front of them, reduce the antagonistic atmosphere with humor. Or attempt to temper the immediacy of an attack by inviting the other person to meet with you privately and/or at another time. Hold your temper, and instead of becoming defensive, try agreeing with the person. That's right, agreeing with her. The conversation might go like this:

> Boss: This is the fourth time in a row you've been late with the marketing report. It's clear you don't care about other people's priorities.

> You: I can see how you might think that, Jo. But the truth is, we're understaffed. My people have been coming in on Saturdays—without asking for overtime—just to handle everything that's on their plates. Now is probably a good time to ask you about hiring two junior associates so the next report will get in on time.

The first thought that came to your mind when accused of not caring about other people's priorities was probably: "What about *my* priorities?" Or, "You don't know anything about the pressures we've been dealing with." Rather than escalate an already tense situation, though, it's better to try viewing the situation from the other person's viewpoint and then get her to try and view it from yours.

4. Be firm without being offensive. You need not rely on sarcasm or belittling behaviors to make your point. But you will need to nip potentially disruptive or destructive behaviors in the bud. Otherwise, they can get out of hand.

Apologies

Dostoevski wrote about Marmelodov, a character known for compulsively confessing. The management equivalent is the individual who over-apologizes, even for things she hasn't done or hasn't done wrong. Beware of using the phrase "I'm sorry" too often. Even if you have made a mistake, there are other ways to express your regret.

You can take a humorous approach: "Whoops! How did *that* happen?" "There I go again." "Overlook this, please, and you can have all the Snickers I've stored in my top drawer." Or, in a more serious vein, you can apologize without using the word "sorry." For example, "I apologize for that." Or "I didn't mean to do that." Or, "That was not supposed to happen." Or even a question, "Did this cause difficulty for you?"

Consider how General Norman Schwarzkopf dealt with an embarrassing situation involving the president. In a television interview, Schwarzkopf had recommended the continuation of the march against Iraqi forces. This recommendation differed from President Bush's wish to bring an end to the

Gulf War. When push came to professional shove, Schwarzkopf's apology was simple and straightforward; he expressed his regret that "a poor choice of words" on his part might have resulted in dishonor cast upon the president. He did not back down from his recommendation, however.

Develop the habit of foreseeing the deep waters into which inappropriate words might plunge you. And realize that true privacy, like true secrecy, is a very rare condition indeed. Know, for example, that your e-mailed words can very easily come back to haunt you. Know, too, that things you share "in confidence" are usually not kept that way very often.

Consider David Brinkley, who may be remembered more for his comments on his final Sunday morning news show than for all the comments he made in the fifteen years he hosted it. He chose to apologize to President Clinton on that show for informal remarks he made about the president on election night. The words were well-crafted, but Brinkley no doubt regretted that he even had to express them. He shared with an audience of millions something he had written years before: "It may be impossible to be objective, but we must always be fair." Brinkley explained that he was tired the night he accused the president of being boring and uncreative. He acknowledged that he had been both "impolite" and "unfair" in his observation. And then he apologized.

If you've made a mistake, apologize for it. Be sincere in your apology. Don't attempt to minimize the consequences of your mistakes. Don't point out that everyone else does it. Don't try to blame others. Instead:

- Apologize as soon as you can after the faux pas and move on.

- Avoid trying to excuse your behavior with weasel words.

- Give a sincere explanation.

- Appeal to the good nature and sense of decency possessed by those whom you may have offended. After all, no one is perfect and we all make mistakes from time to time.

- Know that your salvation lies in truly trying not to make the same mistake twice.

OVERCOMING OBJECTIONS

The Ben Franklin divide

One of the simplest and most effective ways to overcome objections is to use the Benjamin Franklin technique. This Philadelphia statesman found that the best decision soon becomes obvious when the situation choices are described in terms of pluses and minuses. This technique works with influencers and decision makers alike. All you need to do is take a sheet of paper and draw a line down the middle. Write a plus sign at the top of the left-hand column and a minus sign on the top of the right-hand column. At the very top, write down a situation in which you hope to influence someone to accept an idea you are proposing.

Now get to work, listing all the advantages of the proposal on the left and all the reasons why the person might object on the right. Ideally, your left-hand list will be considerably longer than your right-hand list. If is isn't, the disadvantages of the proposal may outweigh the advantages. Your proposal in this case should be reworked before it is proposed.

The third step requires you to focus on the objections likely to be raised. For each, write a fact or statistic likely to make the objection seem less "objectionable." By anticipating the resistance you will probably get, and by having an answer ready for each negative that is cited, you will walk into the influence situation prepared for victory.

Situation: Currently, there is no wellness program at work. I'd like to persuade my co-workers to join me in a program that includes walking at lunch, eating more fresh fruit and vegetables, taking vitamins, flossing more regularly, and so on.

+ Advantages	− Disadvantages
Improved health	1. Don't have time
Greater vitality	2. Takes too much effort
Increased camaraderie	3. No budget for this
Lower medical claims	
Reduced stress	
Reduced need to hire temps	
Workload more equitable	
Prizes for team with lowest cholesterol	
Improved self-esteem	
Greater productivity	
Ability to gain info from other places with such programs in place	

Information to offset objections

1. We are given an hour for lunch each day. We could walk for half an hour and eat during the other half. Or we could walk a whole hour every other day. Flossing and vitamins we could do while we're "on hold." We could have fruit at staff meetings instead of donuts.

2. We're all adult enough to know there's no pain, no gain. In fact, we probably teach such a value to our children. If we are not taking care of ourselves now, we're going to experience a whole lot more pain in the future. These programs can be fun. In fact, 91 percent of employees at Florida Power and Light rated their wellness program as "important."

3. It doesn't cost anything to walk, to quit smoking, to floss, etc. In fact, your grocery bills will probably be smaller if you're buying fruit and vegetables and chicken instead of red meats, ice cream, and potato chips. If we do have prizes, we can use petty-cash money.

Knowing the opposition

In addition to knowing the arguments that will probably be offered in opposition to your proposal, you can add to your preparedness by knowing something about personality types and the communication styles to which people respond best. If you are attempting to influence one person, as opposed to a "mixed bag" of personality types, determine what sort of person you are dealing with and communicate in the manner recommended below.

The Scientific Methodical—This type of person tends to be serious, detail-oriented, and orderly in both her thinking and her behavior. Because she prizes analysis, you will need to give her time to process the information you are presenting. It is easy to overwhelm the Methodical, and so you may want to present your idea in stages.

Which of your colleagues fit this description? _____
_____
_____

The Bottom Liner—These are people who do everything in double-time, including their thinking. They move quickly, they talk quickly, they process information quickly. They are no-nonsense people who expect you to be definite, precise, and deliberate. Circumlocution on your part will mean loss of respect on theirs. Deliver what you have to say in the leanest and cleanest way you can.

Which of your colleagues fit this description? _____
_____
_____

The Divergent Thinker—Such individuals will be generating new possibilities for your plan before you've even finished laying it out. Your partnering skills are vital in dealing with a divergent thinker because—even though she doesn't intend to—she may take over the project by the sheer force of her creativity. Jot down her ideas so they are not lost, but don't allow her to sidetrack you or your proposal with her enthusiasm. Review everything that's been discussed before ending the meeting and leave her with a written outline so that she can continue letting her ideas incubate and ultimately mesh with your own.

Which of your colleagues fit this description? _____
_____
_____

The chart that follows will assist you in planning your strategy to overcome opposition.

Name of Colleagues who are: Methodical	Adjectives to Keep in Mind	Best Approach to Use
_____ _____ _____ _____	Exact, accurate, values data, more easily convinced by statistics, prefers a logical presentation.	Present an overview. Then, in stages, lay out the points.
Bottom Line _____ _____ _____ _____ _____	Fast decision maker unwilling to be bogged down by too many facts, prefers to know key points needed to make a decision.	Present the pro's and con's. Let them choose without further input.
Divergent _____ _____ _____ _____ _____	Quick-thinking, often humorous, sees the big picture, does not like routine, easily excited by ideas.	Appeal to their love of the new, different, and unusual.

WRITING WRONGS

Managers who use integrity to influence do so in both their written and spoken communications. A simple checklist will help your documents conform to high standards of both ethics and effectiveness.

■ *Is your point clear at the very beginning?* Your reader/listener should not have to hunt for it. Make your argument persuasively but don't manipulate the audience by burying information they need to know.

■ *Have you organized the information?* Disjointed information creates a negative impression of you and wastes the reader's (or listener's) time.

■ *Have you made a balanced presentation?* Withholding information your reader needs is dishonest, a veritable sin of omission. While you want to make a strong case for your position, you also want to be fair so your reader can make an informed choice.

■ *Have you used statistics?* Disraeli may have been right when he grouped statistics with lies, but when used judiciously, statistics can make a powerful persuasive point.

■ *Have you made a personal appeal?* Statistics alone won't convince. In fact, research shows that sharing a personal experience can be more effective than simply using data.

OTHER MEANS OF INFLUENCE

Whether or not you are aware of the messages you are sending, they are being transmitted nonetheless. Remember, you cannot *not* communicate. Everything you say, everything you do communicates something about you as a person and you as a manager. In what ways are you influencing others?

Think about the following questions. Then, once you've recorded your answers to them, ask your team members the same questions in reference to your views. Privately, compare their answers to yours. If you find yourself being surprised by the discrepancies between the two sets of answers, you may need to rethink the messages you are deliberately or inadvertently communicating.

1. What is your work philosophy?

2. How is it made evident?

3. What are your beliefs about diversity?

4. What specifics reveal your beliefs?

5. What one statement captures your feelings about teamwork?

6. What do you do to lend weight to those feelings?

7. How do you think the average person feels about his or her job?

8. What are you doing to improve or sustain those feelings?

IF YOU WANT TO BE REMEMBERED

Given the fact that the average employee will have 10.3 job changes in a lifetime of work, according to the Bureau of Labor Statistics, the words you speak today may easily outlast you on the job. There are ways to make yourself verbally memorable. Recent research from The Nierenberg Group of New York City (reported in *HR Fact Finder*, December 1998, page 8), reveals that interpersonal communications is the number one workplace skill professionals need as they move into the twenty-first century. What you say and the way you say it is likely to have a lasting impact—either positive or negative—on those with whom you work.

Think not just twice before you speak or write but several times. As you drive in to work, plan what you will say or write in the important personal or written exchanges you have scheduled for the day. Then, when you arrive at work, outline what you plan to communicate to others one-on-one or in a group. Finally, convert the rough draft to the actual remarks you have to make that day. In doing so, you maximize your opportunities to be remembered.

PREVIEW

The next chapter explores the many faces of trust: How we use it to make a difference, how we earn it, how we return it to others so an empowered workplace becomes more definitive than descriptive.

 **TRUST**

It's relatively easy to make money, rules, friends, plans, and schedules. It's considerably more challenging to make a difference. The best managers are professionally schizoid: they are making a difference in the way work is done. At the same time, they are maintaining the status quo. They recognize and optimize strengths. Simultaneously, they identify and remediate weaknesses.

MAKING A DIFFERENCE

Why have you decided to become a manager or team leader? It's a question for which you probably have several answers. One of them may be "the opportunity to make more money." Another one of your answers is probably "the opportunity to make a difference." To make a difference, of course, you need the support and trust of others. And others need to trust you.

It's not as easy as you think to develop trusting relationships. America has become a nation of skeptics. We are skeptical of the motivations of our governmental leaders, our educational leaders, and sometimes even our religious leaders. In fact, in a recent Gallup poll on the issue of public trust, the military was given a trust rating of 64 percent, the police 58 percent, and religious leaders only 57 percent. Journalists, it was learned, are trusted half as much as the clergy, but twice as much as lawmakers.

As a leader of people, you have to earn the trust of those you expect to follow you or follow your directions. They will be waiting to see if you live up to your words. What are the words you use? The following examples about rumors, new hires, and retirees illustrate how two different sets of words can make the same point either positively or negatively.

	Trust-enhancing	Trust-eroding
Rumors	There are a lot of rumors circulating right now. As soon as I can confirm or deny them one by one, I'll put out e-mail announcements. Check your e-mail at least twice a day.	There are a lot of rumors circulating. Believe half of them.
New Hire	Sheila Johnson will be joining our team on Monday. I trust you'll make her feel like part of our corporate family.	Sheila Johnson will be joining our team on Monday. Treat her the way you treat each other and she'll be ready to quit on Tuesday.
Retirement	Bob Tayback will be retiring on July 1. Please join me in wishing him well in his new venture.	Bob Tayback will be retiring on July 1. Of course, he really retired two years ago. He just never left.

As a general rule, use sarcasm at your own expense, not at the expense of others.

EARNING TRUST

Making your staff feel they matter in the grand scheme of things is vital. You can accomplish this in ways that go far beyond financial rewards. Ask yourself how often you do the following:

How often? (S = seldom; O = occasionally; F = frequently)

1. _____ Make promises and then keep them.
2. _____ Recognize others.
3. _____ Share knowledge.
4. _____ Include staff in decisions.
5. _____ Interact with staff on a personal level—e.g., ask about their children.
6. _____ Try to make work more interesting.
7. _____ Praise staff to my manager.
8. _____ Relieve stress via social events.
9. _____ Share credit.
10. _____ Say, "How can we avoid this mistake in the future?" instead of "Who made this mistake?"
11. _____ Offer lagniappes (small rewards people don't expect).
12. _____ Share my values and vision.
13. _____ Give feedback on job performance.
14. _____ Encourage the input of ideas.
15. _____ Discuss career paths.
16. _____ Encourage self-development among staff members.
17. _____ Rotate staff attendance at meetings I have to attend.
18. _____ Extend a human touch (e.g., pat on the back, handshake).

As knowledge grows, so will either trust or distrust. Think of it this way: if a stranger approached you and asked, "Do you trust me?" you would probably say no. In fact, it would be foolish to trust him because you don't know him.

Trust is actually a two way-street. The more you get to know someone, the more certain you are regarding how much trust to accord him. As a manager, especially a new manager with less than three years' experience, you can determine your degree of trust in one of two ways:

1. Start off trusting everyone with 100 percent confidence they will do the right thing. Then as time reveals the extent to which they cannot or will not do the right thing, subtract trust-percentages accordingly.

2. Start off trusting no one. As you learn more about their capabilities and work ethic, you mete out appropriate amounts of trust until you reach 100 percent with each person.

Your staff, of course, will be doing exactly the same thing. They will either trust you implicitly and then revise their position if they feel they are betrayed. Or, they will wait and see how you perform and then apportion trust as you demonstrate how worthy of it you are.

Experienced managers, those who have worked with their staffs for more than three years, have a different set of problems. Typically, trust issues have already been resolved. However, as change and perhaps even crises impact the workplace, the trust levels can shift, depending on how you conduct yourself in each of these circumstances.

EMPOWERING THROUGH TRUST

Definitions

Delegating to your staff or team members is different from empowering them. Delegation is more like a one-way street, with the manager giving directions "from the top down," so to speak. Delegation is more limited in both scope and duration than empowerment. Essentially, you are asking, when you delegate, that an employee take charge of a task and see it to completion. He may not ever do that particular task again.

By contrast, employees who have grown into empowerment—with your assistance—are in a permanent state of awareness, self-confidence, and pro-activity. They have demonstrated competence, earned your trust, and shown a willingness to take on new tasks. Empowerment is more of a two-way street: you can empower your staff to take responsibility, but they might also empower themselves. For example, the secretary who arranges for a police officer to deliver a lunchtime lecture on personal safety is acting in an empowered fashion. Ideally, she will have told you of her project, but because your approval is not required for such a venture, she may not have.

Competence

Deciding whether or not to empower your staff and then deciding how much power to give is not easy. Two determinations must be made: How capable is the person of doing the task you want to authorize him to do (or that he wants authority to do)? Secondly, how ethical is the person? In other words, how much do you trust him? A competent person who is "morally challenged" will probably do the organization little good. And a person who is morally sound, but lacking skill, similarly might cause more harm than good.

How can you determine the level of empowerment that exists in your workplace? It's simple: just ask each staff member to write a number from 1 to 5—with 1 representing "minimum empowerment" and 5 indicating "maximum empowerment." Then meet with them one-on-one to discuss the numbers they recorded. There may be good reasons why some wrote low numbers. For example, if an employee is new to the organization or new to your department, he should not be fully empowered until he has learned how things are done and until you have learned exactly what he is capable of doing.

Once you've established how much empowerment each individual has, believes he has, or wants, you can meet with the staff as a whole to discuss the factors impacting low empowerment and those relating to high empowerment. You can also discuss empowerment opportunities with them.

Integrity

A good communication system, established early in the empowerment process, will help you avoid problems later on. It can help develop trust as well. And it will help you identify integrity issues so that each party understands what constitutes an ethical fulfillment of agreements. Assuming the employee wishes to accept or initiate an empowerment project, questions like these need to be raised and resolved.

■ What is the exact scope of the project?

■ What deadlines are involved?

■ What is the budget for this project?

■ Has necessary approval (budget and other) been obtained?

■ How much time will be required?

■ What resources are needed?

■ What could go wrong?

■ Who will be impacted?

■ What notification has been given?

■ Are legal/OSHA/union issues involved?

■ What needs to be put in writing?

■ What degree of monitoring should accompany which empowered actions?

■ What decisions will be made by the employee?

■ What decisions fall into the supervisor's realm?

■ What are the possible consequences of the transfer of power?

■ What is the best possible outcome?

■ What are the manager's expectations?

■ What are the expectations of the person being empowered?

Responsibility

Before you can give employees the freedom to act as they see fit, you have to work with them to determine levels of responsibility and authority. With those who lack confidence, are new to the team, or who are not interested in becoming empowered, you may wish to propose relatively short-term and uncomplicated assignments. If empowerment can be viewed on a continuum:

Minimum   Moderate   Maximum

then such individuals—at least initially—should be given minimal empowerment. As their confidence grows, they will move along the continuum.

There will be other employees who, by virtue of the time spent with the organization or by virtue of their experience and expertise, will want to be fully empowered. They are eager to step out of restraining position descriptions, determined to step up to the line at which challenges are being passed out. Empowerment, of course, means greater opportunity: opportunity to treat the job as if it were their own business, opportunity to grow, to learn, to exert greater control over the decisions that impact their job.

Your responsibility is to explain exactly what is meant by "power to the people." You may have to define terms and boundaries, establish a reporting procedure and deadlines, specify what is expected to be done by whom by when. If you are used to speaking in generalities, if you have been heard to utter empty phrases like "Do whatever it takes," then you may have to revamp your linguistic style if you want empowerment to work. Otherwise, your employees will be kept in the dark, where dissatisfaction grows at a mushroom pace. You'll have to trust that employees will not give away the store. You may even need to assure others that empowerment is not at all akin to "turning the asylum over to the inmates."

To be sure, employees in an empowered environment have responsibilities as well. They are expected to look for ways to continuously improve, to offer suggestions, to volunteer, to give input to problems and decisions facing the team or department as a whole. Some employees are reluctant to accept greater responsibility because they feel they were not hired to do anything beyond their job description. As a manager, you have to respect that feeling and not foist empowerment upon the individual. To do otherwise defeats the purpose of empowerment and may make your motives suspect.

At the same time, however, you will want to work directly and indirectly with empowerment-reluctant individuals to demonstrate the many benefits they can acquire by taking on new opportunities. Depending on the prevalent attitudes in your department, there may be some employees who feel that headquarters has all the answers (or operates as if they do). Thus, when they hear about empowerment, they suspect headquarters is setting them up to fail. Another type of employee believes it is easier to follow instructions than to make decisions. This way, if they fail, they can blame the person who directed them. They know that in an empowered culture, they may be that person and so they shun empowerment possibilities.

Assess your empowerment expertise

To explore which empowerment-levels are best for which situations, take the following quiz. For each scenario, place an "X" somewhere on the continuum line to indicate how much empowerment you would give to the groups involved.

1. You are a new supervisor. The person you replaced was extremely popular, partially due to his "hands-off" policy. He essentially left people alone to "do their own thing." The problem now is that they are used to this freedom and you've learned that some of the "things" they are doing conflict with the organizational mission.

| Minimum | Moderate | Maximum |

2. You are the leader of a department that is cooperative with you and with each other. You've often commended them for working so well and working so well together. They meet their deadlines, they take pride in their work, they possess the esprit de corps necessary to cope with daily demands as well as the occasional crisis. You've been asked, because of special training you have received, to spearhead some "headlight" projects with your staff.

| Minimum | Moderate | Maximum |

3. "Self-starters" is the perfect word to describe the members of your team. They have worked together for several years and function well together. The levels of both trust and respect are quite high. Two members of the team, however, are quite reserved. You wish they were a bit more assertive.

| Minimum | Moderate | Maximum |

4. You trust your staff members implicitly. Over and over, they have demonstrated high-quality work as well as commitment to the organization. A wonderful opportunity has presented itself for all of you: the head of the organization has asked that your team participate in a special pilot project.

| Minimum | Moderate | Maximum |

Compare your answers

1. At least at first, you have to take charge of this situation by granting a Minimum level. It's already out of hand and you don't want it getting worse. Remember, you have not been hired to win a popularity contest but rather to get the job done. And it's clear the job is not getting done if staff members are ignoring the mission. Once everyone is on board, so to speak, *then* you can back off and grant more Moderate or perhaps even Maximum Levels of empowerment.

2. The scenario states that you have been given special training but the others have not. Therefore—until they all understand just what "headlighting" means—you will be the one in charge and the Minimum level of empowerment will be most appropriate. As soon as everyone understands as much as you do about this topic, then the staff can operate at Moderate or Maximum levels of empowerment.

3. You're fortunate to have a staff like this. It makes your job easier. In terms of the empowerment level to be given to the group as a whole, Maximum is the answer. They are working beautifully and need no further involvement on your part. Let them be. If you are truly concerned that some staff members are too introverted, work with them individually.

4. Because you will be participating in the special pilot project—as opposed to turning it over to the staff entirely—the Maximum Level is not the best choice here. They alone will not be entirely responsible for the results. Instead, that will be a shared obligation and so the Moderate Level is the one that will engender involvement from all concerned.

Characteristics of an empowering manager

Robert Eaton, CEO of Chrysler, was recently asked how his company managed to increase earnings by 246 percent to a level of nearly $4 billion. His reply: "If I had to use one word, it would be 'empowerment.'" His quote alone is sufficient reason to begin sharing power if you've not already done so. (Perhaps you think your workplace is empowered; a reality check might prove otherwise.)

Place a checkmark in front of the following descriptions that apply to the way you manage.

- ❑ I share power willingly.

- ❑ I subscribe to the statement by General George S. Patton: "Give direction, not directions."

- ❑ The question for most of my team/staff members is not whether they wish to be empowered, but rather how much empowerment they wish to have.

- ❑ My team equates empowerment with opportunity.

- ❑ As a rule, my staff members solve their own problems instead of running to me for help with every problem that arises.

- ❑ My team regards problems collectively, rather than viewing them as difficulties for the organization or for me to deal with.

- ❑ The team believes that leadership does not belong exclusively to those at the top.

- ❑ Staff members take initiative.

- ❑ Ideas are offered unsolicited.

- ❑ It's recognized that the people closest to the process understand the process best.

❑ Staff members act as "intrapreneurs," operating as if they themselves owned the business.

❑ Team members are clear about which decisions they can make "on the spot" and which need to be brought to my attention.

❑ Certain policies, practices, and procedures must remain inviolate, no matter how much empowerment team members have. They know what cannot be altered.

Having six or more checkmarks suggests that you have met some success in establishing a climate in which trust can flourish. If your staff is clear about the rules they can bend, the rules they can change, the rules they can throw away altogether, and the rules that must remain sacred, then you are free to concentrate on the higher-level responsibilities for which you were hired.

Characteristics of empowered employees

You can use the following checklist in any number of ways: To evaluate how your manager works with you; to assess how your team as a whole operates; to determine the relationship you have with each of your team members; to encourage staff members to explore their own levels of empowerment. In addition to checking off the descriptors that apply, you may wish to get even more explicit: write a number between 1 (low) and 5 (high), reflecting the extent to which the description fits the individual(s) involved.

_____ Is assertive

_____ Is committed

_____ Is prepared

_____ Trusts leadership of the organization

_____ Does not need to dominate every situation

_____ Is goal-oriented

_____ Receives deserved recognition

_____ Has a vision

_____ Is considerate

_____ Believes in the democratic process

_____ Is flexible

_____ Works harmoniously with others

_____ Is open-minded

_____ Is honest

_____ Is customer-focused

_____ Is willing to accept accountability

_____ Has and uses ground rules

_____ Pitches in, even when not asked to do so

_____ Contributes to meetings

_____ Can be trusted

_____ Seeks harmony

_____ Asks for what he or she needs

_____ Is creative

Throughout this chapter, you have been encouraged to engage in some introspection, examining the degree to which you trust others and the degree to which you are empowering them, based on that trust. If you've come to the realization that some things need to change, you will want to take the time to plan your action before executing your action plan. There is little point in undertaking improvement initiatives in one area if another area would have a bigger payoff. Make certain the areas you've targeted for improvement truly need to be improved. Check with others at levels above and below your own before embarking on your improvement journey.

Trust-driven empowerment works—studies show improvements in quality, service, and productivity, with gains of 50 percent and higher, when employees are empowered to do what they believe is the right thing to do.

PREVIEW

Chapter 5 covers persuasion by appropriate means. This includes political correctness, at the heart of which is respect for others. Appropriateness also covers the content and context of persuasion messages, extending to electronic media as well.

◆5◆ APPROPRIATENESS

The business cemetery is filled with the gravestones of managers whose poor judgment led to inappropriate words or actions. The best possible advice you'll ever receive is to think before you execute those inappropriate words or actions. At the heart of inappropriate or politically incorrect actions is a lack of respect for others. Keep uppermost in your mind the need to treat individuals and situations with dignity and professionalism. This simple guideline will help you avoid the fatal errors others have made.

Respect can be demonstrated in both micro and macro fashion. For example, if you simply ask, "Is this a good time?" before engaging someone in conversation, you are acknowledging that their time is as valuable as your own. On a larger scale, the respect can be shown via your everyday managerial style.

POLITICAL CORRECTNESS

Take this quiz to learn the extent of your self-control, a critical factor in correct, respectful communications.

		Yes	No
1.	Do you consider others your equal, no matter what their position?	___	___
2.	Do you consciously pride yourself on the things you didn't say?	___	___
3.	Have others told you, more than four times, that you are tactful?	___	___
4.	Can you actually feel yourself getting "heated" during verbal conflicts?	___	___
5.	Do you verify your understanding of the other person's viewpoint before presenting your own?	___	___
6.	Do you deliberately rely on facts rather than emotion in a confrontation?	___	___
7.	Do you rehearse in advance of a potentially difficult encounter?	___	___
8.	Do the majority of your interactions end on a positive note?	___	___
9.	Are you known for maintaining grace under pressure?	___	___
10.	Do you refrain from bringing up the past in order to win an argument?	___	___

Tally your "yes" answers. If there are more than eight of them, you have already uncovered many of the secrets of effective and appropriate communication. If, however, you are "diplomatically challenged," consider softening your basic style. The words you use to express consideration of other people will never come back to haunt you.

CONTENT AND CONTEXT

Content

The English language has over a million words, unlike other languages, such as Papiamento, which has under 1,000. As a result, the number of choices available to you for the expression of a single thought are infinite. The manager concerned with appropriate verbal choices is aware of the flexibility of language. Short case studies follow, some based on famous figures, others based on the unknown. For each, decide which response is most like the one you would have made. When you've finished, turn to the end of the chapter to learn what reply was actually given.

A. You are at dinner at your boss' home. He has asked you to say grace, which you proceed to do. Suddenly, he interrupts: "Speak up, Bill," he demands, "I can't hear a d _ _ _ thing you're saying."

Your likely response would be:

    1. "I'm sorry, sir. I'll speak more loudly."

    2. To continue as if you hadn't heard the boss' interruption.

    3. "I wasn't addressing you, sir."

B. Your boss has an organization-wide reputation as a perfectionist. He is now asking you to redo something you feel is perfectly acceptable. You feel you have more important things to do.

Your likely response would be:

    1. "I don't really think it needs revision, but if you want me to revise, I'll do it."

    2. "I can do what you want. And then you'll be happy. But I won't have time to do the variance report by the first of next month. And then you *won't* be happy. Which is the more important priority for you?"

3. "There's nothing wrong with this the way it is, Jon. I'm not going to do it over."

C. You have just listened to an absolutely unworkable proposal from one of your staff members. You don't want to discourage future suggestions, but at the same time you don't want him thinking the idea has merit.

Your likely response would be:

1. "Persuade me."

2. "Thank you, Jerry, for bringing this to me. It's an interesting concept, but I just don't think we can put it into effect."

3. "Let me think about it, Jerry."

D. You have never had to deliver bad news of any sort to Bobby. Today, however, it is your job to report that an application for promotion has been denied. You fear the worst and your fears, you soon learn, are well founded.

Your likely response would be:

1. "Don't get mad at me. It wasn't my decision."

2. "I was passed over three times myself before finally getting this position."

3. "Why don't we talk about this tomorrow?"

E. You have a Lone Ranger on your team. His work is extraordinary but his personal isolationist policy is affecting morale. You're meeting in private now and he's just asked if you can fault anything about his work. Of course, you can't.

Your likely response would be:

1. "There's more to work than work, Jay."

2. "Sometime's I'm reminded of Casey Stengel's remark that it's easy to get good players but getting them to play together is the hard part. Jay, you're undeniably good but I need you to spread some of that goodness around."

3. "It's not your work I'm talking about. It's your attitude."

Context

You can demonstrate respect and consequently appropriate communication behaviors in a great many ways. Directness and consideration are not necessarily mutually exclusive. Sometimes, because of the pressures of time, we just jump in and say what has to be said, do what has to be done. Nike's exhortation to "Just do it" has extended to realms far beyond the athletic. In these turn-of-the millennium times, managerial actions are perhaps best reflected in the three-word dictum stressed by Jack Welch, CEO of General Electric: "Speed, simplicity, self-confidence."

But while there is much to admire in this style of operating, you need to—occasionally at least—consider the possible downside of such efficiency. Not all communication exchanges are created equal—some need much more finesse than others. Some require much more planning than others.

The planning may include the context of the exchange. In other words, decide which medium you will choose for conveying your message: electronic, written, spoken, telephonic. The time of day will matter, as will the location of the one-on-one interaction. Context refers to the many factors surrounding the delivery of the words you will use. Planning also includes content, the actual words that are used in the interaction.

Check off the contextual tools on the next page that you typically use in an appropriate manner to demonstrate respect.

❑ *Listening.* Do you demonstrate respect with good listening, or do you merely attempt to force your ideas on others without waiting for feedback?

❑ *Tone of voice.* Do you consciously choose a matter-of-fact tone, or are you allowing abrasiveness to creep in?

❑ *Interruptions.* Do you refrain from comments until the other speaker has reached an appropriate stopping point, or are you prone to jumping in and possibly causing him or her to lose his train of thought?

❑ *Gestures.* Is there alignment between your words and your gestures, or is there a mismatch? For example, When you say, "I am not angry," are you pounding the desk?

❑ *Time.* Do you typically respect it and use it appropriately? (For example, a delayed apology is usually half as effective as one offered immediately after the flare-up.) Or do you speak or write with little thought to timing?

❑ *Silence.* Do you use silence by choice to convey a specific message? Or are you using it in a way that might be understood? (With a chronic complainer, for example, silence might be interpreted as agreement.)

Ideally, you had at least three checks, which would suggest that you are deliberately making good decisions regarding the use of contextual tools in your communications. If not, spend at least ten minutes a week (perhaps with some assistance) analyzing ways to improve your nonverbal skills.

E-MAIL ETHICS

Couple the ease of electronic communications with the fact that companies employ fewer secretaries than ever (more than a half-million secretarial jobs have been eliminated in the last decade), and you're left with a mountain of E-mail. Lest you're tempted to hope the E-mail explosion is replacing paper communications, though, consider this: According to the Environmental Protection Agency, Americans used 7.1 million tons of paper in 1993. As the century turns, we are using 8.5 million.) Even if you don't have a secretary to screen incoming mail and even if you like the feeling of being sought out, you can control the amount of mail you receive and respond to.

1. If your organization/office doesn't have a policy stipulating E-mail use, form a committee and write one. With a million messages moving along Internet lines every hour, and with the number of e-mail lawsuits growing, companies need to keep employees informed about proper use. They should know, for example, that even after messages have been deleted, certain software can recapture those deleted thoughts. They should also know that all it takes is one employee using organizational E-mail illegally and the government can seize the entire computer system to preserve evidence.

2. Set limits. Specify certain periods during the day for sending or reading E-mail. Otherwise, you could find yourself being drawn by its magnetic pull the whole day long.

3. Establish channels. Designate specific people to receive specific types of communications and then refrain from cc'ing the world.

4. Use the telephone, memos, teleconferences, and in-person meetings, as appropriate, instead of E-mail. E-mail compliments, for example, seldom compare to praise delivered in person.

5. Restrict E-mail messages to legitimate organizational concerns. Avoid using the medium to gossip, to complain, to opine, or to vent emotions.

6. Keep messages short and pertinent. If the reader has to scroll to find the point, you've probably digressed unnecessarily.

7. Periodically, caution staff members about rumor-mongering, the results of which grow exponentially when E-mail is used.

8. Re-read the message before pressing the "send" button. It's not the proofreading errors that cause trouble but rather the content and the tone of messages.

9. Try to respond to E-mail messages daily. If you are traveling, arrange to have your mail forwarded.

10. While the matter of privacy regarding E-mail and other computer files has still not been settled in the courts, it's a good idea to spell out the corporate policy on this issue.

Online networks

The Internet allows you to make friends, influence people, and be influenced in return—all with merely a few clicks in a few seconds. Not only can you establish cyberspace connections that will provide you expert advice at virtually no cost, but you can also widen your customer base, learn what's happening in your industry, conduct surveys, and explore business opportunities. If you find a post that reflects your own feelings on certain issues or a post that appears to have been written by someone with extensive experience, you could reply publicly or privately to that person. A more personalized message—rather than a public posting—will more likely permit the formation of a professional association with the individual.

Joining forums that encourage such networking means abiding by certain rules of netiquette.

1. If you belong to online forums or listserv groups, "lurk" for a week or two before posting a message. This way, you can get a feel for the nature of the messages and the needs of the message-posters. You'll also know what discussions have already been explored.

2. When giving your opinion on electronic networks, be cautious. Certainly, you are entitled to freedom of speech, but should your speech cross into libelous areas, you may find yourself facing a lawsuit.

3. Make certain your posting states, usually in the signature line, that the opinions you are expressing are your own and not your organization's.

4. If you receive information from an online colleague, you will have to decide if you wish to thank him via e-mail. Some people feel that sending a message of appreciation only clutters up the recipient's mailbox. Others feel that such messages are always welcome. You'll have to decide for yourself, but be guided by this question: If you send "electronic expertise," would you want to be thanked?

E-Democracy

Technology has effected a certain democratization within organizations. At Microsoft, for example, you don't have to be a vice-president to electronically chat with Bill Gates. Hierarchical frameworks are being replaced by infrastructures that no longer resemble pyramids. Among the terms used to describe these power-decentralized systems are phrases like "pizza-pie," "clover-leaf," and "starburst." "Blueberry pancake" is the metaphorical term used by the CEO of VeriFone, Hatim Tyabji.

Tyabji regards self-directed work teams as the blueberries, each of which functions independently in solving its own problems, establishing its own policies. Extending the metaphor, he tells staff members that all blueberries are created equal. Tyabji encourages self-reliance; he advises employees not to expect headquarters to have the answers. There are no secretaries at VeriFone—the company operates electronically, 100 percent electronically.

Such structural shifts present both danger and opportunity. The influential manager is taking measures now to offset the dangers and optimize the opportunities.

VOICE-MAIL VALUES

Legend has it that after President Rutherford Hayes installed the very first telephone in the White House in 1878, the very first words he spoke were "Please speak more slowly." Too-rapid speech on voice-mail messages is but one of the ways we negatively impact each other's productivity. Playing phone tag is another. Yet another is being engaged in conversations that wander aimlessly. A fourth is the power of a ringing phone to interrupt your concentration. And, of course, a phone that goes unanswered or a voice-mail message that goes unreturned can harm your reputation for efficiency.

Before considering improvements to your incoming and outgoing voice-mails, consider this question:

As far as the workplace is concerned, what do you most value?

1. _____

2. _____

3. _____

4. _____

5. _____

Now consider how some of those values could be incorporated into your use of voice-mail. For example, if you answered "professionalism" as one of the things you value, ask yourself and your staff if the recorded messages on their voice-mail reflect professionalism. The information should be clear, succinct, and somewhat formal in tone. It should provide necessary information, such as who the caller can contact if you are out of the office. "Cute" works for Barbie dolls, not for office communication systems.

If efficiency is another thing you value, listen to your voice-mail messages. (If possible, ask a colleague whose efficiency you respect to listen as well and offer you feedback.) Does your recorded message give details a caller would need? For example, does the message encourage the caller to leave a detailed message rather than just announce his name and number? In the same vein, when you leave a message on someone else's voice-mail, do you tell the purpose of your call? Do you note the best time for reaching you so telephone tag can be avoided?

These tips may guide you in applying your listed values to the inbound and outbound calls you receive and make. Invite your staff also to consider continuous communication improvements.

Incoming

1. Your recorded message should state your name, the department, and the date.

2. It should ask the caller to be specific in his request.

3. If you are out of town, mention that and note the name of someone else who can help.

4. If you are simply unavailable for a short time, tell what the best time would be for reaching you.

5. If you anticipate receiving a number of calls seeking answers to a specific question, give that information in your recorded message. For example, "If you are calling about registration for the upcoming conference, you can obtain the forms at our Web site. Or just leave your fax number, and we will fax the registration to you."

Outgoing

1. Identify yourself and your organization when leaving a message on another person's voice-mail.

2. Clearly and specifically state the purpose of your call. Do this right after giving your name and company so the recipient can determine its priority.

3. If a return call is unnecessary, state that as well.

4. Advise the person of the best time to reach you if he needs to do so.

5. Thank the person for his attention to your request.

6. Spell your name or at least repeat it slowly.

7. Repeat your phone number.

8. Don't leave multiple voice-mail messages. If you don't get a return call in a few days, try sending an e-mail or letter instead.

ANSWERS TO CONTENT: CASE STUDIES

Take another look at the case studies on pages 93 and 94, and then read the recommended replies below. In your own circumstances, of course, a different reply might be more suitable.

A3 was Press Secretary Bill Moyers' way of giving a firm but diplomatic response to President Lyndon Johnson's intrusive comment during grace.

Perfectionists have a strong need to be in control. In question B, answer #2 gives the supervisor that choice and does so in mildly humorous fashion. It also protects the manager should he be accused in the future of being late with the report.

You don't want to always play the role of hatchet-man. But you also don't want to offer false hope. The first answer to question C allows the idea-proposer to explore the unfeasibility of his own proposal.

Shifting the blame to others is both cowardly and unprofessional, and shifting the discussion to a later time doesn't take care of the problem at hand. The best choice for question D is, #2, to reveal your own, similar, painful experience. People often take rejection very personally, but it's a universal experience.

Most people respond to sports references, especially if there's a bit of humor involved. Answer #2 for question E simultaneously acknowledges the employee's contribution and stresses exactly what the problem is.

PREVIEW

The next chapter will cover the style and substance of influence overtures. It emphasizes that your style of managing, like your style of communicating, should conform to the requirements of the moment. Too rigid a style will not permit you the flexibility required to manage in these "nanosecond" times. Also examined are ways to establish *koinonia*, the spirit of fellowship. Finally, the workouts popularized by Jack Welch at General Electric and the need to remain flexible are explored in Chapter 6.

◆6◆ STYLE

IT'S BEEN SAID THAT what you say equals what others will do but *how* you say it may well determine how well they do it. Your style of managing, like your style of communicating, is a combination of content and context. Consequently, it will both remain consistent and yet change with the circumstances.

This is not as paradoxical as it may seem at first. To illustrate, the "what" or content of both your managerial and your influence style is a well-known constant. The "how," though, is a variable. In other words, your style may include a results-driven approach. But the words/actions you choose to show that style will be impacted by certain factors.

Consider this simple analogy. You would never wear a tuxedo to a business meeting, nor would you wear shorts to a funeral or a gown to a picnic. Your wardrobe is large enough to accommodate various demands. Your management and influence "wardrobes" should also be large enough to accommodate the various situations in which you find yourself on a daily or weekly basis.

THE STYLES OF INFLUENCE

Flexible Management Styles

Research conducted by Professor Fred Fiedler of the University of Illinois found that most successful managers respond to three elements—the nature of the work, the nature of the individuals, and the nature of the situation—before choosing the management style to fit the circumstances. If you do this, you are subscribing to what he calls the Contingency Style of Managing.

Another way to view his theory is to regard management as a continuum, with the Autocratic style at one end and the Laissez-faire ("Leave-them-alone") style at the other. In the middle is the Participative style. The decisions regarding styles of managing parallel the decisions regarding empowerment that we explored in an earlier chapter. Then, as now, numerous factors must be considered.

| Autocratic | Participative | Laizzez-faire |

If you were asked to place an "X" on the spot that marks your typical style, you would—ideally—have a hard time defining your typical style. That is because your style would conform to the situation at hand. So, if you were supervising new hires, your style would be different from the style you'd use with veteran employees. It would appear more on the left side of the continuum than on the right side, which favors a laid-back style, appropriate for the veterans.

Similarly, if you were dealing with a crisis, your style would be more demanding than democratic or participative. During team meetings, if you function as a team member and not the team leader, your style becomes a participative one.

Which styles do you use under what conditions?

Style	Conditions
1. Autocratic	_____
Autocratic	_____
2. Democratic	_____
Democratic	_____
3. Laissez-faire	_____
Laissez-faire	_____

Flexible Influence Styles

Since you were a child, you have altered your expression to suit the needs of different individuals, different occasions. With teachers, your language choices were probably more formal than the casual expression you adopted with your friends. You probably spoke differently in church than you did with your siblings. This verbal flexibility carried over quite naturally to your high school or college circumstances. Terms papers you wrote had a decidedly different tone from the notes you wrote home or to friends.

The very same ability to conform is called for in the world of business, particularly in view of the rapidity with which change occurs. Consider for just a moment these predictions by futurists:

- Because English is the language of choice for more than 85 percent of the computer users in the world, futurists predict the disappearance of most other languages.

- Because technological terrorism is not labor- or capital-intensive, world-watchers foresee increased attacks on information systems and infrastructures.

- Because the Internet does not recognize geographic boundaries, employers are hiring "electronic immigrants," international telecommuters who can respond easily and well to job demands.

- Because online learning can be delivered so affordably, schools and universities and training programs as we now know them will disappear.

- Because technology is streamlining diagnostic procedures, experts predict that more than 4,000 genetic diseases will be controlled and even eliminated only twenty-five years into the new century.

These and other startling advances will have worldwide repercussions. The face of business will have more than metaphorical nips and tucks. It will be completely reformed and reshaped in the years to come. Consequently, it is critical that we accept, cope, and benefit from change.

Among the characteristics that should describe your flexible management style are these words: adaptive, speedy, simple, and self-confident. The latter three are the ones stressed repeatedly by Jack Welch of General Electric.

Adaptive

Ideally, you are the kind of manager who will not permit past successes to become future failures. That is, you rely on the skills that brought you where you are, but you know if you do not add to those skills, you are doomed to stagnate. Consider the case of the CEO who was trained as an engineer. By the time he has reached the executive level, he depends less and less on engineering principles and more and more on management principles. You need to let go of who you are—to some extent—in order to become who you want to be.

Clearly, the world will not wait for you to decide if you want to advance with the times. Change will occur, whether or not you support it. And to refuse to support it is often to commit career suicide. To find your Adaptability Quotient, answer "True" or "False" to the following statements.

1. _____ When vacationing, I prefer to return to places I've enjoyed rather than explore new places.

2. _____ I work best under challenging conditions.

3. _____ I can abandon my plans if something better presents itself.

4. _____ In general, I think our society relies too much on traditional ways of doing things.

5. _____ I believe many of the world's problems can be solved by "down-to-earth" individuals rather than visionaries.

6. _____ I would enjoy an exotic adventure, like exploring the rain forests in Brazil.

7. _____ If stimulation doesn't occur on a regular basis, I create my own.

8. _____ I enjoy a good debate, even if the issue isn't very important to me.

9. _____ I try to lead life "in the moment," in the here-and-now.

10. _____ I don't like wasting time.

Interpreting your score: Generally speaking, the fewer "correct" answers you had (zero to three), the less inclined you are to change. The more correct answers you had (eight to ten), the more adaptable you are to change, perhaps even inclined to create it where it doesn't exist.

While there is nothing wrong with being truly set in your ways and nothing wrong with being addicted to change, either extreme could spell trouble. If your score fell in the range of four to seven correct answers, you are basically content with your life and your job. Nonetheless, you enjoy doing things that are challenging. You have a balance in your life and show it via the combination of routine activities (at home or on the job) and stimulating activities (at home or on the job). You adapt to changing circumstances readily—you are not overanxious about the future nor do you feel an unacceptable need to take risks or seek thrills.

In terms of your influence style, you may be regarded as too cautious if you scored at the low end. You probably are doing more managing than leading, more maintaining of the status quo than implementing innovation. If you scored at the high end, you may be initiating change simply for the sake of initiating change. A score in the middle suggests a good balance between the two responsibilities of exemplary managers: managing the existing circumstances while simultaneously seeking to improve them.

Answers: 1. F   2. T   3. T   4. T   5. F   6. T
           7. T   8. T   9. T   10. T

Speedy

The nanosecond nineties are giving way to the demands of the new millennium. While we had the luxury of lengthy deliberation in the days before faxes, e-mail, flash technology, and videoconferencing, today we are often forced to make quick decisions and produce quick results by virtue of our very accessibility to others. Past players in the great game of business operated as chessplayers do. Today, business-world residents play a different kind of game altogether—more like a high-speed video game than a game allowing time for deliberation.

If you are moving at a turtle's pace on a road dominated by high-speed engines, you are in imminent danger of becoming managerial road kill!

Answer "True" or "False" to the following statements in order to acquire some sense of your Speed Quotient.

1. _____ Many people think of me as being "always in a hurry."

2. _____ I know I am impatient.

3. _____ I am easily bored.

4. _____ I could not work for a company like General Electric, where the vision statement describes a culture that hates "bureaucracy and all the nonsense that comes with it."

5. _____ I often have to go back and correct mistakes I made the first time around.

6. _____ I'm not very good at paying attention to details.

7. _____ I like the feeling of having five things going on at once.

8. _____ I am often prevented from accomplishing what needs to be done because I am waiting for others to get back to me.

9. _____ I am uncomfortable making quick decisions.

10. _____ I frequently make "gut" decisions.

Interpreting your score: Again, there is danger in the extremes here. Moving too slowly (few correct answers) may cause others to lose confidence in you and may even cause you to lose opportunities. Moving too quickly may jeopardize your position. When it comes to problem solving and decision making, at least consider the negative consequences hinted at by Norman Mailer—"There's this faculty in the human mind that hates any question that takes more than ten seconds to answer"—and by H. L. Mencken—"For every complex problem, there is one solution that is simple, neat . . . and wrong."

Ideally, you were in the middle in the number of correct responses you had: five or more indicates you are able to respond to the urgencies of the moment. Nine or ten correct answers, though, may mean you are rushing to judgment about matters that require more deliberation.

In terms of your influencing style, be guided by circumstances. With critical demands, you may indeed have to make snap judgments. With trivial or nonconsequential matters, you should. But when you have important but not urgent matters to consider, invite others to be involved in the decision-making process. Set limits, however. Tell them in advance how much time will be allotted to discussion and tell them the due dates you've established for special goals to be met.

Answers: 1. T   2. T   3. T   4. F   5. T   6. T
          7. T   8. F   9. F   10. T

Simple

American jurist Oliver Wendell Holmes once commented, "I would not give a fig for simplicity this side of complexity, but I would give my life for simplicity the other side of complexity." There's good simplicity and there's bad simplicity. As he noted, simplicity that emerges from an intense study of complex issues is good. When statistician W. Edwards Deming, for example, was able to explain variation on a level a child could understand, he achieved the simplicity born of absolute comprehension of complex issues. But someone who made simple statements without having given the time complexity demands would be guilty of bad simplicity.

Effective managers keep things simple, especially in their communications. Learn your Simplicity Quotient by answering "True" or "False" to the following statements.

1. _____ A sentence can be effective even if it has only one or two words.

2. _____ Effective communicators employ sentences of various lengths.

3. _____ Business writing should be on a 12th grade level of readability.

4. _____ A good way to begin a business communication is with these words:

    "It is the purpose of this memo to advise you that. . ."

5. _____ Storytelling is more impressive than statistics in getting a message across.

6. _____ Paragraph length should be consistent.

7. _____ Big words reflect advanced education and so are preferable to little words.

8. _____ A computer spell-check program eliminates the need for proofreading.

9. _____ World and national leaders often use sentences with only three words.

10. _____ Sentences in business correspondence should average about twenty words.

Interpreting your score: If you study the masters of verbal simplicity, you will find certain threads running through the common fabric in which they cloak themselves. Those threads are reflected in the statements above (and their correct answers below). With this assessment, the greater number of correct answers you had, the more successful you are likely to be in influencing others with a style that is both simple and significant. If you scored well, you are probably using the most efficient medium for expressing your messages. You understand, in all likelihood, which "how's" can best deliver select "what's."

Answers: 1. T   2. T   3. F   4. F   5. T   6. F
           7. F   8. F   9. T   10. F

Self-confident

It is nearly impossible to lead others when you doubt yourself. How is managerial self-confidence manifested? In any number of ways. In the support you give to your staff. In your willingness to share credit. In the frequency with which you take a stand. In your ability to propose ideas and make them reality. In the way you speak. To obtain your Self-Confidence Quotient, answer "True" or "False" to the following statements:

1. _____ I do not need to hear the opinions of others before venturing my own.

2. _____ I believe my life is more "externally" controlled than "internally" controlled. (In other words, most of the things I do are in response to the expectations of others, rather than in response to my own decisions.)

3. _____ When faced with self-doubt, I actively take time to remind myself of past accomplishments.

4. _____ Being around people who dress better, have more education, and earn more money makes me uncomfortable.

5. _____ When I hear criticism, my first thought is to devalue its importance.

6. _____ I am not a very creative person.

7. _____ I am consciously working toward specific goals.

8. _____ I have several relationships that validate my sense of self.

9. _____ My view of myself is accurate, based on the feedback I receive from others.

10. _____ I could be called more of a "control freak" than "someone who is in control."

115

Interpreting your score: When the ancient Greeks advocated moderation in all things, they were establishing guidelines for millions of people, for thousands of years. If you had a "moderate" score, with four to seven correct answers, you have probably found an approach to managing others that is neither too hesitant nor too brash.

If you only had a few correct answers, you may be playing too cautious a role. Perhaps you've had negative experiences that have caused you to withdraw. Perhaps you are uncomfortable taking a firm stand. Perhaps you see no need to stand out. Keep in mind, though, that others are expecting you to go out on a limb, at least once in a while. It is this admirable trait of challenging the status quo some anonymous wit alluded to when he observed, "Every great oak was once a nut that stood its ground."

Of course, it is possible that your self-confidence borders on the arrogant or aggressive. And if you had eight, nine, or all ten correct answers, you may indeed have too much of a good thing. Do some self-assessing. Ask yourself if your relationships with staff members are comfortable or if you, perhaps, are putting them off. Are you respected by your own managers or are you regarded as a loose cannon or as a self-promoter?

A moderate number (four to seven) suggests you can control a potentially strong personality so that teamwork causes the job to get done, not the force of you or your position. With answers in this range, you are likely to be sufficiently self-confident to inspire others without dominating the circumstance.

In terms of your influence style, balance a healthy desire for open expression with an equally healthy willingness to remain open to the ideas of others.

Answers: 1. T   2. F   3. T   4. F   5. F   6. F
           7. T   8. T   9. T   10. F

THE SUBSTANCE OF INFLUENCE

It's been observed that every time you open your mouth or put your thoughts on paper, you allow others to see inside your psyche. Do you agree? If not or if you're not certain, take a look at this statement, which a job candidate gave in response to the question, "Why did you leave your last job?" His reply? "Because they made me a scapegoat, just like my previous three employers did."

It's only one sentence and yet it affords extensive insight into the "victim" mentality this person has. Is he likely to get the job for which he is applying? Not very. Our words reveal all kinds of things about us. And sometimes we are not even aware of what we are radioing to others, with signals loud and clear. A good example is contained in the following question. "With what sort of person do you *least* like to work?"

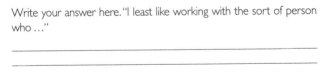

Write your answer here. "I least like working with the sort of person who ..."

_____

_____

_____

Psychologists will tell you that whatever answer you gave, you are probably the opposite of that personality type. To illustrate, if you indicated you do not enjoy working with people who are lazy, you are probably quite industrious.

There's another simple way to gauge the traits you value. What ten people come to mind as soon as you read this question:

Whom have you met, heard about, or seen within the last six months that stands out in your mind?

1. _____

2. _____

3. _____

4. _____

5. _____

6. _____

7. _____

8. _____

9. _____

10. _____

Next, for each person, record the one thing that made him or her so memorable. What do you remember about that person?

1. _____
2. _____
3. _____
4. _____
5. _____
6. _____
7. _____
8. _____
9. _____
10. _____

These ten traits are probably quite close to the things you value or the *opposite* of the things you value. So if someone stands out in your head for being extremely knowledgeable, it's a pretty safe bet that you value learning. On the other hand, if you remember someone who was extremely rude, chances are you yourself value kindness and treating others with respect.

Now that you've established some core values, you can examine your own communications to determine if these values are reflected in the substance of your interactions with others. Try the following exercises to learn if they are.

1. Gather five to ten pieces of correspondence that you've written in the last several weeks. Analyze each and underline the substantive values that are implied or directly stated in your communications. If you can find few or none, consider how the correspondence *could* have been written to reflect some of your core values.

2. With the knowledge and permission of co-workers, ask to tape record some of your exchanges. Then go back and listen to yourself intently. If you hear core values revealed in your interactions, commend yourself. If not, work on improving your communication skills so that both content and context reflect the precepts you believe in.

PREVIEW

Top-of-the-line responses to bottom-line questions will be covered in the next chapter. So, too, will the encouragements to Dialog, Inquire, Respond, Environ, Contact, and Tie Up, which constitute the DIRECT Approach. Finally, the sins and scintillas of sugar-coating will be explored.

 **IMPACT**

If you are influencing effectively, your words and actions alike are having a positive impact on others. They are being remembered long after they have been spoken or performed. Let's use the simple example of introductions. Often at meetings for an interdepartmental project or in training sessions, you will be asked to introduce yourself. Most people say something like this: "Hi. My name is Susie Smith and I work in Accounting and I've been with the company for six years."

There is nothing actually wrong with this kind of introduction except that it is bland. It makes no impression on others. It does not impact their consciousness. Contrast it with an introduction like this: "I'm Susie Smith and I can make sure this team completes the project on time and within budget!" Certainly more memorable, but a tad aggressive, you think? Not really. Susie, after all, was chosen to be part of the team for the contribution she can make. And even if some people had a somewhat negative first impression of her self-confidence, within the hour that impression would be offset by Susie's subsequent words and actions (assuming, of course, she is sincerely interested in contributing to the team and not in self-aggrandizing).

TOP-OF-THE-LINE RESPONSES TO BOTTOM-LINE SITUATIONS

There is no doubt about it—being a manager means being a motivator. And while many believe you cannot motivate others because they have to motivate themselves, the issue is really a semantic one. Think of it this way: Have you ever been motivated to do better by another person—a minister, perhaps, like Reverend Billy Graham or Reverend Jesse Jackson? Has a humanitarian ever moved you to donate to a charity—a humanitarian like Mother Teresa or Princess Diana? Has a world figure ever prompted you to write to Congress or to support a cause—someone like Colin Powell or Jimmy Carter? If you answered yes, then you know that great influencers can motivate. And while your own influence may not be great, the truth is you can and do motivate others to greater accomplishment.

While management has its downside—difficult people and difficult situations—there is an upside as well: the fact that you are not the only manager in the history of time to have faced these difficulties. The very fact that they are repetitive offers hope—someone else has already met these problems successfully. From the common body of managerial experience, we can learn and derive benefit.

The situations that follow happen in virtually every office or shop floor at one time or another. We'll examine some time-tested responses that will help you in coping with them.

Situation:

You have a *whiner* on staff, someone who doesn't even bother to hide his dissatisfaction with the workplace, with management, with the world at large. While most everyone ignores his comments, in the aggregate, they are beginning to affect morale.

You approach needs to be firm yet understanding.

Response:

"Paul, I think you know the importance of teamwork. I think you also know much we value what you contribute to the team. But it seems lately certain things are bothering you. Let's see if we can examine those in some detail. I'll do what I can to make them less of a problem for you."

Situation:

You have an *angry customer*, disturbed about the way a sub-ordinate has handled a problem. He has demanded to speak with you. It's important that you support your staff member while supporting the client at the same time. It's not as difficult as you may think.

Response:

"I appreciate your bringing this problem to my attention. As you know, Tony has offered to repair the directional signals. And he was correct in explaining to you that our normal policy does not include making a loaner car available to you while such repairs are being made. However, because this is the third time you have had to bring the car in for the same problem, I'm going to make an exception to our basic policy. If you can get a ride in before 5 this afternoon, we'll have the loaner car ready for you."

Situation:

As a quality advocate, you know the importance of having
staff members suggest ideas for improvement. You also know
when they stop suggesting, apathy has overtaken interest.
However, Roberto continues to make *numerous but unworkable suggestions*. The challenge before you is to get him to
think through his proposals before submitting them.

Response:

"American businesses are sometimes criticized for hiring
employees' hands and not their heads or their hearts. Such
criticism could never apply to you, Roberto. You've actually
been averaging three suggestions a week. From this point on,
though, I hope we can aim for quality, rather than quantity.
Your ideas so far have been submitted raw. I suspect that as
they come to you, you jot them down and turn them in. The
problem is that I don't have time to research their feasibility.
And so I've not been able to give them the attention they
deserve. Nor can I turn them in to upper management in their
current form.

"Would you be willing to still record all your ideas but do
some screening before turning them in? At the end of each
week, choose the idea most likely to succeed. Then flesh it
out—maybe gather some data—before turning it in. That
way, I can forward it as-is to my manager right away and
we'll see where it goes from there."

Situation:

More often than you like, you are in a position of *telling
someone he didn't get the promotion* he was expecting. Once

you tell him, he will be expecting something else—a sound rationale that makes him understand why decisions were made that weren't in his favor. To do this without evoking anger is challenging. To do it without evoking anger yet still offering promise requires extraordinary persuasive skill.

Response:

"Three times in my career, Isaac, I've been passed over for a promotion I thought I deserved. What I felt then is probably what you are feeling now—disappointment and perhaps even bitterness. I got over my initial feelings of rejection, though, when I was able to look at the situation objectively. In time, I realized I truly wasn't the best person for the job. In this case, the interview committee was very impressed with your experience, your background, and the way you conducted yourself during the interview. But in all honesty, there was one candidate whose experience was just a little broader than your own, whose skills were more extensive.

"I hope you will apply the next time a promotional opportunity comes up. In the meantime, if you are interested, I'd be willing to work with you to close the gaps that now exist in your resume."

THE D-I-R-E-C-T APPROACH

Most employees appreciate a supervisor who speaks to them directly, who "tells it like it is," who refuses to play games or to keep agendas hidden. You no doubt pride yourself on exhibiting such behaviors. But as a believer in continuous improvement, you no doubt realize there is always room for improvement. The steps in the D-I-R-E-C-T approach should help you attain those improvements.

Dialogue

The communication equation allots you 50 percent talking and 50 percent listening in your interpersonal exchanges. If the ratio goes too far beyond this, it is really not an exchange but more of a one-sided domination. Depending on the nature of the exchange, you can use questions to encourage true dialogue. Of course, you must then listen to the response you've elicited.

Periodically stop, for example, and ask the other person, "How do you feel about what I've said so far?" or "I'd really appreciate some feedback from you at this point." You can also use simple prompts to elicit more information, such as "Please tell me more" or "Isn't that like a project you managed a few years ago?"

Inquire

Some communicators simply "plop" knowledge in front of others, without establishing a setting or segue for the receipt of that knowledge. By using certain lines of inquiry, you can build a framework that makes your reader or listener more receptive to the information you are about to present. To illustrate, "John, do you remember how much time you spent determining our primary performance measures?" A question such as this is bound to hook the other person.

The inquiry can occur at any point, of course, not simply at the beginning of an interaction.

You can periodically ask, "Am I making sense?" or "Is this clear or would you like another example?" At the end of the interaction, you can inquire about the person's readiness, willingness, and ability to perform the task or execute the assignment. "Can you foresee any problems, John?" is one good inquiry. Another is, "When would you like to meet again for a progress report?"

Respond

Consider the wide range of responses available to you— silence, questions, short affirmations, and full-blown replies. You also have the range of written, oral, telephonic, and electronic responses from which to choose. Adding more to this array is the fact that for any given message you have to convey, there are hundreds of ways and several hundred thousand words waiting for your selection.

Clearly, the more sensitive or important the communication, the more carefully you must make your choices. As you make your choices, recognize that not all words have the same meaning to people. And, there are certain words that may suggest bias, whether or not you intend them to do so. As an example, consider this sentence with and without the word "again."

> "I see that you've signed up for computer training."

> "I see that you've signed up for computer training again."

The addition of that simple word implies there was little or no need for the employee to have done so, unless, of course, he failed to grasp the fundamentals the first time around. In either case, the implication is an insulting one and suggests a bias of superiority on your part. Weigh your words carefully—they have the power of balms and bombs.

Environ

To "environ" is to "surround." Consider the circumstances surrounding the communication—especially if the news is not good. Your consideration might include physical, emotional, personal, environmental, or people-related factors. Among the questions you'll have to answer are these:

- Should I speak with staff members one at a time, or meet with them all at once?

- What time of day is best for delivering this news?

- Which day of the week is best?

- Should anyone else be present?

- Should the meeting be here at work or at an outside location?

- What material should accompany the delivery of this news?

Even when the news is good, you may wish to give some thought to the setting. For example, if someone on your staff is being honored by the media for his volunteerism, you will probably want to recognize him at work as well. As you plan the small celebration, consider questions on the people-related level, such as,

- Who at the executive level should be invited?

- Would the employee's parents enjoy being present? If so, will someone need to pick them up?

- Would the employee's wife appreciate an invitation?

- Should the children be included in the event?

- Is it possible to have a photographer from the company news-letter present?

- Should the celebration be a surprise or should the employee be told about it in advance?

Contact

The more complicated, difficult, or sensitive the information you have to convey, the more contact you'll need with the person involved. Contact in the D-I-R-E-C-T approach is made in three stages. Your initial contact, the pre-meeting phase, will simply provide the details about the upcoming meeting. The more serious the issue, the smaller should be the interval between the initial contact and the actual meeting. In fairness to the other person, who will perhaps be facing a disciplinary action or even a termination, don't let more than a week intervene. The person will no doubt be worrying; you don't want to prolong the agony.

Give as much information as you can. If it is an informal meeting, say so. If it is more serious, advise the person so that he can have a union steward or perhaps even legal repre-sentation present. For your part, you may wish to have a mediator or arbitration official at the meeting as well.

At the actual meeting, establish some human contact, such as shaking hands at both the beginning and end of the meeting. Personalize the meeting, no matter how awkward the circum-stances, by offering a beverage. Have paper and pencil ready also (and possibly a box of tissues) should they be needed during the discussion. It's often a good practice to jot down what was agreed to, make a copy, and have both of you sign and date the document.

At agreed-upon times, meet again to see what progress has been made toward resolving the issue discussed at the actual meeting. If you find indications the employee is working toward this goal in good faith, don't hesitate to express your appreciation.

Tie-up

Seamstresses know that if they don't tie a knot in their final stitch, all the work they've done will unravel. By extension, successful influencers know that the loose threads of conversation need to be tied up before the interpersonal exchange is terminated. At the conclusion of a team meeting, for example, the effective team leader will summarize what has been done and what has yet to be done, by whom, and by when.

Especially in telephone conversations that have veered off the business path to discuss more personal topics or even unrelated topics, it is important to re-state purpose before ending the communication. A simple sentence such as, "Well, then, I can look forward to receiving that index in the next day or so."

SUGAR-COATING: SINS AND SCINTILLAS

Managers walk a fine line between truth-telling and feelings-protection. Techniques that may have worked in the past are not always usable today. For example, you may have learned that the sandwich technique is a good way to deliver negative news. With it, you start by noting positive actions your subordinate may be engaging in. Then you would transition to the real point of the exchange—the delivery of carefully couched criticism. You would then finish the "sandwich" with another positive slice.

Many employees object to such a ploy. Just as criminals can see through the good cop—bad cop routine police officers used so often in the past, today's workers barely hear the opening positive remarks because they know the negatives will be forthcoming. It's better to deal kindly, firmly, and directly with the problem facing the two of you.

Sins

The sandwich technique is one of the sugar-coating sins managers can commit in their sincere desire to communicate effectively. A comparable sin can be found in the blizzard of false concern used by telemarketers worldwide. An example follows.

Telemarketer:	Good evening, Mr. Jones. How are you doing tonight?
Mr. Jones:	Fine.
Telemarketer:	My name is Phil Johnson and I'm with LawnLovely, a premier company dedicated to making beautiful lawns like yours even more beautiful.
Mr. Jones:	How do you know I have a beautiful lawn?
Telemarketer:	Well, you have been identified as a person with discriminating taste who cares about the appearance of his property.
Mr. Jones:	And who has identified me?

| Telemarketer: | People who care about the appearance of their property know how important it is to have properly seeded and properly weeded grass. |
| Mr. Jones: | Who identified me? |

| Telemarketer: | We have a special going on right now for new customers. For only $99, you can have ... |
| Mr. Jones: | Could you please stop reading the script and answer my question? |

| Telemarketer: | Ummm ... what was the question? |
| Mr. Jones: | Who identified me? |

A loud click is heard and the call is disconnected.

How much more refreshing it would be to simply have the telemarketer say:

"I'm Phil Johnson with LawnLovely and we want your business!"

Scintillas

There are times, of course, when you do have to soften the blow of harsh realities. Sugar-coating is perfectly acceptable under such conditions. Sugar-coating could be compared to what they say in the world of time management: "Be ruthless with time but gracious with people."

Depending on the circumstances, here are some scintillating ways to sugar-coat the bitter pill of reality, making it easier to swallow.

■ "The last three times you made this request, we were able to accommodate you. This time, we simply don't have the personnel available."

132

- "I can't give you a free transfer, but I can take 10 percent off your first order."

- "I can make this a one-hour presentation instead of a full-day program, but that might make participants feel too rushed. Can we either eliminate some of the topics or else do a half-day program instead?"

- "I know you've been out of the office because of foot surgery and you were probably forced to catch up on things without taking your usual care. But the last report you submitted did not reflect your typical thoroughness. Please do it over, even if it means getting it in a week or ten days late."

- "The points you made about reevaluating job descriptions were valid. In fact, they were persuasive. But we won't be able to allocate time this year for the project. So, for the very last time, I promise, we'll have to base merit raises on the existing descriptions. But next fiscal year, there will be a closer alignment between what is actually being done and what is actually earned."

- "I'm flattered you thought of me to head the charity drive this year, Isaac. It took me a while to decide whether or not to accept the honor. But I've decided I can't—not with the back problems I've been having and the time I've been putting in to learn the new software systems. Thank you, though, for thinking of me."

- "I understand what you're saying here, Juan. And I agree—we definitely need better equipment and additional staff members. I'm not saying 'no.' I'm saying I need a better budget justification. Begin by recording data on the existing operations—we can use those as leverage."

- "They say the best things in life are free. But they also say there's an exception to every rule. Here's the exception. I'd like to describe the best time and attendance system you'll find anywhere in this county. But it's not free. However, once you see its full rolling accounting of employee work hours and watch how it automatically measures present discrepancies, I think you'll agree it pays for itself."

■ "I could do exactly what you're asking. But I'm afraid that's not the best use of my time. I can get the entire layout done in five days, but if you assign me the editing instead, it'll probably take me seven days. I'm just not as strong in that area as I am in the assembly. But whatever you finally decide will be acceptable."

PREVIEW

The Integrity Gauges presented in the next chapter offer clear and concise guidelines for use in situations that you've not encountered before. Also covered is the ROR-Shock Model, with its emphasis on Reality, Openness, and Reification. Finally, in its exploration of manipulation, Chapter 8 shows you how to apply the Win-3 Test in situations that test your ethical stance.

8 MANIPULATION

You'll be asked to suspend judgment as you read this chapter on manipulation. Typically, this word has negative connotations. We think of manipulative individuals as being somehow unethical, even though the dictionary defines the word as "skillful handling or operation, artful management or control." The verb is defined as "to manage or control artfully or by shrewd use of influence." Admittedly, one could both use influence shrewdly and use it unethically as he manages. But the word, in and of itself, is a neutral term.

Manipulation from which you derive advantage is perfectly acceptable. Truly, there is nothing wrong with considering your own needs first. In fact, you have been doing that since you were born, when you screamed for me-first attention for your needs, oblivious to the needs of others. Ideally, you've moved beyond such win/lose scenarios to develop Win/Win outcomes. Problems arise only when you operate from a position of personal advantage *without* taking the needs of others into account. Such behaviors constitute unethical manipulation.

Salespeople know that "hard closes," which are more concerned with the seller's need to sell than the prospect's need to buy, seldom work. It's been estimated that fewer than 5 percent of such situations result in actual sales, and of those that do, nearly three-quarters are subsequently cancelled or returned when the buyer experiences remorse.

Unethical influence is simply not worth the effort, damage to your reputation, potential loss of customers or supporters, nor the decrease in your self-respect. You will almost always know, deep down, the difference between ethical and unethical influence. You really are your own best judge of ethical behavior. After that, those with whom you work provide a good sounding-board for actions that are or are viewed as ethical and unethical. The integrity gauges that follow should help you in making judgments about those difficult situations in which the cost of doing the right thing may be very high indeed.

INTEGRITY GAUGES

Typically, the easiest and fastest way to gauge whether a particular action is ethical or not is to ask a question or a series of questions. For example, let's say you are in the middle of writing out checks to pay some personal bills during the working day, and the following question occurred to you:

> ▮ If the customer could see what I'm doing right now, would she be willing to pay for it?

You would probably catch yourself and put the checkbook away.

Most of the integrity issues you face as a manager are cut and dried, black-and-white questions for which there is either precedent or guidance in the form of the values with which you were raised. But sometimes loyalties conflict or the foundation of your values crumbles in the face of new knowledge. In such circumstances, the following questions will help set standards for acting and reacting with integrity. They will help find the truth to which author Elie Wiesel alludes, "I have one request: May I never use my reason against truth."

- What action would be most consistent with my values?

- With whom could I discuss this decision?

- What would be best for the organization?

- What action would have the least negative impact on others?

- Would this show respect for my own abilities?

- How might this action be construed or misconstrued?

- Would I be willing to accept complete ownership of consequences?

- What is the right thing to do?

- What would my choice reflect about my values?

- Who would profit most from this decision?

- Could I bear the losses that might result from this decision?

- What options do I have?

- What do I deserve to have happen?

- How will others view me if I make this decision?

- If my child faced this problem, what would I advise him or her to do?

- What is fair?

- What is the ideal way to resolve this dilemma?

- How will I feel tomorrow if I do this today?

- What would the person I most admire do in these circumstances?

What other questions have you (or others) used as a lighthouse to steer you in the often-turbulent moral waters? Record at least five here. Continue adding such questions and keep them in a notebook to which you can turn when those gray areas challenge your gray matter.

1. _____
2. _____
3. _____
4. _____
5. _____

THE ROR-SHOCK MODEL

Designed to shock you into recognizing feasibility and then to make you roar with approval as you convert current conditions to ideal ones, the ROR-Shock Model is based on the observation that the impossible is often the unattempted. In this section, you are asked to begin by describing an existing reality in your workplace, but a reality that you'd like to improve. What one thing or situation do you feel would have the greatest positive impact on people or productivity if it were resolved or improved? Describe that current reality here.

The one thing I would most like to improve is _____
_____
_____
_____
_____

Next, let's do an assessment of that reality, your openness to changing it, and your willingness to begin the process of "reification," during which you make things happen.

Reality

The following assessment will give you some idea of your actual feelings regarding the situation you've just described and the possibilities of remedying it.

> **Directions:** Read the statements that follow each parenthetical label. They relate to both the specific situation you've described and your general attitude about making positive change. Select the one that most closely represents how you feel today, as you are reading these statements. Circle the number next to the statement. (Should you feel two statements equally apply, circle both. Do not circle more than two, however.) Read all the statements in the group before you make your selection.

Reality

1. (Optimism)
   - 0   This is an impossible situation.
   - 1   I can simply expect to live with this until I retire or until some other major event occurs.
   - 2   I think there is a way out of or around this situation.
   - 3   I have solved equally difficult situations in the past.
   - 4   I am confident I can make this situation better.

2. (Accomplishment)
   - 0   Most of the time, I regard myself as a failure.
   - 1   Even someone with twice my experience could not resolve this problem.
   - 2   It would be easier to resolve this if I had dealt with it before.
   - 3   I take pride in my accomplishments, of which I hope this will be one.
   - 4   I generally have a do-or-die philosophy.

3. (Decisiveness)
    0 I don't like making decisions at all.
    1 When it's absolutely required, I can and will make a decision.
    2 I know the decision precedes the accomplishment.
    3 I can usually "undo" incorrect decisions I've made.
    4 I generally believe that if nothing is ventured, nothing is gained.

4. (Contentment)
    0 It's easier to just avoid dealing with this situation.
    1 I don't have enough energy to cope with this.
    2 I think the situation could be improved but I wish someone else would do it.
    3 I am spending more time than I should worrying about this.
    4 I will not be satisfied until I've resolved this.

5. (Self-Esteem)
    0 Deep down, I don't like myself very much at all.
    1 I have very few things in my work that I can point to with pride.
    2 I think the manager's job is a very difficult one.
    3 I periodically congratulate myself for what I've done so far.
    4 I thrive on dealing with situations others would describe as impossible.

Openness
1. (Acceptance)
    0 There is nothing I can do about the way things are.
    1 This is my lot in life—to bear up under unbearable situations.
    2 I may not be able to do this alone, but I can make the situation better.
    3 I acknowledge the power of cooperative effort.
    4 I really believe people can change and so situations can change for the better.

2. (Challenge)
    0 This situation won't change, so why should I waste any time on it?
    1 I feel overwhelmed by the effort it will take to make this better.
    2 I know such problems go with the territory.
    3 I look forward to the day when I have achieved my goal to improve this situation.
    4 I actually welcome tough problems because they make me tougher.

3. (Receptivity)
    0 There is little point in trying anything new. Nothing will work in this case.
    1 I tend to rely on strategies that have worked well for me in the past.
    2 The balance between using what I know works and experimenting with something new is about fifty-fifty.
    3 I not only solicit the advice of other people when I have a problem to solve, I actually use it.
    4 My bag of managerial strategies is constantly being revised.

4. (Tolerance)
    0 I am so burned out I feel I cannot take this situation any more.
    1 I am angry with the individuals involved in this situation for failing to see what they are doing wrong.
    2 I basically have a "laissez-faire" or hands-off style of management.
    3 I understand and respect the different views that people have, but this situation is having a negative impact on our mission.
    4 I believe some good comes out of every situation and things will be better here once this situation is straightened out.

5. (Flexibility)
   0   I don't like change.
   1   I believe you have to stick to your game plan. Otherwise, why have one?
   2   I'm just as adaptable as the next person.
   3   I agree that "a foolish consistency is the hobgoblin of little minds."
   4   I have no problem adopting someone else's plan if it's as good as or better than my own.

Reification
1. (Success)
   0   I'm known for starting things and never finishing them.
   1   If others don't prod me, I tend not to get things done.
   2   I complete the things I am expected to complete.
   3   I am internally, rather than externally, driven.
   4   Once I've begun something, I have a strong need for closure.

2. (Risk)
   0   I'm afraid to try things I've not tried before.
   1   I think people who call themselves visionaries are usually self-indulgent and rash.
   2   I dislike routine.
   3   I find a certain degree of exhilaration in working on new projects.
   4   I have enough self-confidence to know that the things I undertake usually turn out well.

3. (Consequences)
   0   One reason I don't like to try new things is that I fear I'll get in trouble.
   1   There are some people who would like to see me fail with this situation.
   2   If I felt more secure about my position, I would be willing to experiment more with possible solutions for this problem.

    3 I don't mind delaying temporary pleasures now to reach a more permanent goal later.

    4 My manager supports my efforts, even when I make mistakes.

4. (Future)

    0 I worry a lot about getting in trouble for decisions I've made.

    I I hesitate to start something new because I don't want to make waves.

    2 I will be favorably regarded if I can resolve this situation to everyone's satisfaction.

    3 I am quite satisfied with where I am and what I have.

    4 I feel very optimistic about what the future holds in store.

5. (Initiative)

    0 I am not nor do I want to be empowered.

    I I would describe myself as having a cautious nature.

    2 I would be willing to go out on a limb to resolve this situation.

    3 I subscribe to the suggestion that if something is not broken, you should break it.

    4 I've often been described as a self-starter.

Total of all circled numbers: _____

Interpretation

The higher your score, the more likely you are to help produce beneficial outcomes for yourself and others. A score of 45+ reveals both self-confidence and determination on your part. You know that obstacles are necessary aspects of performing the managerial function. Because you take such a positive approach, others probably gravitate to you, hoping to be included in the tough work that will virtually guarantee the ultimate success of the problem you are dealing with.

A score under 15 can be explained by the nature of the situation you have described. It may truly be an impossible

situation or one that has little hope of being resolved successfully. But there is also the possibility that your approach to
problem solving does not depend on influencing others.
Return to your lowest individual scores and consider how
those statements relate to particular aspects of your work as a
manager. If you do regard yourself as a loner, know that lone-
ness is good in some situations, but not all. Let your ROR-
Shock score influence you to influence others toward
collective decision making and problem solving.

If your score falls between 15 and 45, you already have a good
attitude toward creating new realities and are likely to be the
sort of person who makes things happen. You have little
trouble identifying a problem and working with others toward
its resolution. You probably also have a high level of energy
and faith that things will work out sooner, rather than later.

Creating new realities with the ROR-Shock Model

No matter what your score, these recommendations will aid
in defining the reality surrounding a troublesome situation,
remaining open to possibilities, and then taking action to
begin the process of influencing others (and yourself as well)
to create a reality that didn't exist before your collaborative
involvement.

Reality—As discouraging as the circumstance may initially
seem, there is hope in the fact that a number of experts are
out there, individuals who represent your first stop on this
improvement trip. Ask friends, acquaintances, other
managers, and even strangers (on the Internet, for example)
for advice on handling this situation. Don't hesitate to read
books, attend seminars, read articles, watch educational

videos, and listen to audio tapes devoted to the same type of problem you are experiencing.

Once you have a better grip on the reality of the situation—few are truly life-threatening or earth-shattering—then you'll be in a better position to lay out a plan of attack and to persuade others to join you on the journey. You're persuasion efforts will be facilitated by the careful detail you've put into the plan.

Openness—Ideally, it will not come as a shock to you that you have not cornered the market on good ideas. Ideally, you concur with the opinion of literary critic Mark van Doren: "Bring ideas in and entertain them royally. One of them may be the king." To create such a climate of innovation, though, puts special responsibility on your shoulders. If your staff senses you have a need to reign, they'll simply not share their ideas very openly or willingly. It is hoped you can influence them to contribute so the kingly, or at least the princely, ideas can be entertained and then adopted.

Reification—In Latin, "res" means "thing." When you reify, you move from the abstract to the concrete. In so doing, you've begun the process of creating a new reality, a new thing. As you influence others, you'll find that small, incremental successes, duly noted, move projects toward completion and move employees to the next success level.

To solve the difficult reality you described earlier, think of one specific, concrete step that could be taken—not to solve the problem in its entirety but simply to make a declaration that you have begun the solution process. Engage others in attaining this first goal. Celebrate victory in an appropriate way and then move on to the next goal. This is the incremental process known as *kaizen*, which has served so many organizations around the world in their improvement efforts.

WIN-3 TEST

We've become so accustomed to hearing about Win/Win outcomes that we feel satisfied when we've achieved them. The Win-3 Test is a simple one—it merely asks you to identify a third beneficiary of the Win/Win outcome toward which you are striving.

Let's say you've been working with an employee who responds with sarcasm to any and all stimuli. You've been meeting to discuss the effect her words are having, not only on office morale but even on her career. Add one more element to the equation. Ask and answer the question that will allow you to pass the Win-3 Test:

- Who or what else will benefit if this problem is successfully resolved?

Clearly, the employee herself will benefit, long-term, if she is able to mend her verbal ways. And co-workers will benefit as well. Consider who benefits from the third (or fourth, or fifth . . .) win; this will help you explore additional factors that should be taken into account. For example, it really is to *your* advantage to resolve this as quickly as possible because the problem is draining time that could be better spent elsewhere. Another beneficiary might be customers, who just might stop doing business with a representative whose attitude is an abrasive one. The organization itself, of course, could wind up a winner. How? If the environment is not made less hostile, another employee may very well decide to go out on stress leave, thus costing the firm quite a bit.

Contemplating the possible Win-3 outcomes will help you structure the points you wish to make during your influence overtures.

PREVIEW

The next chapter explores the components of change. It also examines the values employers seek and the values employees see and seek. You'll learn too about ways to ethically influence team members and team accomplishments.

 **VALUES**

Author Philip Selznick notes, "The institutional leader is primarily an expert in the promotion and protection of values." As a manager interested in acquiring new ways to manage even more effectively, you probably consider yourself an institutional leader as well. So if Selznick's words carry truth, then it's time to think about the values you promote and protect. And time to think about values as part of the influence process.

Begin by mentally separating your work life from all other parts of your life. Keeping work as an isolated segment, think about what you value as far as your job is concerned. You might, for example, value the fact that your own manager is not a micromanager. So the word "freedom" might be your answer to the question.

■ What do you most value about your job or your workplace?

_____

In respect to the idea you've just listed, reflect on what you are doing or what you have done to promote and protect that value for your staff members.

▪ What steps do you take to make certain that your staff can derive benefit from what you most value?

_____

_____

_____

_____

Each of us, from time to time, needs to be reminded of the good fortune that has been bestowed upon us. Here's what we mean. Have you ever returned home from a trip, complaining about delays, and had a family member remind you that—compared to the fact that the plane did not crash—a delay has very little significance? Such reminders help us place trials and tribulations in their proper place. And that place is always on a lower rung of the ladder of important values.

You can use such reminders from time to time to validate common values. Albert Schweitzer spoke of the need to think occasionally of the suffering of those whom we spare ourselves the sight of. It's easy enough to shove the sights and sounds of tragedy into the farthest recesses of our mind. To do otherwise can be painful. Yet when we do allow ourselves the occasional thought, we simultaneously allow ourselves to feel grateful by comparison.

The very fact that an employee is complaining about work, for example, makes her more fortunate than all the people who are currently unemployed or all the people who are too ill to go to work on a daily basis. Do not be heavy-handed or holier-than-thou when you use such observations. But know you can influence others to appreciate the gifts they have been given. Use references to values in a sparing but significant way.

THE COMPONENTS OF CHANGE

Author Anais Nin may have best captured the reluctance we experience regarding change. In one masterful sentence, she acknowledges the fear preceding change and the fear that follows change: "The risk of remaining tight in a bud is more painful than the risk it takes to blossom." Most of us have become tight in our metaphoric buds. Over the years, we have built layers and layers of self-protective coverings and so find ourselves quite comfortable doing the same things, thinking the same thoughts, meeting the same people.

But there comes a point, as Nin suggests, when remaining ensconced in familiarity can actually hurt us, can actually cause more harm than if we had ventured forth. When you are trying to influence others to accept change gracefully, point out they really don't have a choice about acceptance. The change will occur with or without their endorsement. Their only choice, really, is the decision to adapt with little stress or to fight the change and thus have difficulty with it. These tips might help in your influence efforts.

- Use the change model popularized by psychologist Kurt Lewin. (He is also the author of the Force Field Analysis tool for problem solving.) Before introducing change, Lewin recommends thawing or defrosting or melting down the existing frozen practices or mindsets. In other words, undertake efforts to make imminent change less threatening. Then proceed to make the change. After a suitable period of time has elapsed, re-freeze the new way of doing things. As you institutionalize the change, though, realize that this new standard operating procedure may itself, in time, have to be thawed out as a new way of doing things is introduced.

■ Brainstorm with staff the successful changes they've undergone as human beings, going as far back as moving from a crib to a bed; from remaining prone to sitting up, to crawling, to walking, to running; from staying home to leaving for school, etc. Itemizing the tremendous number of significant changes we have undergone will make the upcoming change fit more easily into the natural order of business practices.

■ Reluctance to change is rooted in fear. But fear of *what*? List here ten specific fears staff members may have concerning an upcoming change.

1. _____

2. _____

3. _____

4. _____

5. _____

6. _____

7. _____

8. _____

9. _____

10. _____

Next, ask staff members to itemize the specific reasons for their unwillingness to change. Compare their answers with your own to obtain a clearer picture of what you need do to allay their fears.

VALUES EMPLOYERS SEEK

Nearly a hundred years ago, Sigmund Freud wondered what a woman really wants. There have been numerous variations on that interrogative theme, including the question of what managers want from their employees. Given the fact that it's not a perfect world and that, consequently, your staff members are doing some things you find irksome, take the following quiz to learn more about yourself.

Directions: Place a checkmark in front of those statements that describe people or situations that bother you.

_____ 1. People who talk too much.

_____ 2. People who come to work when they are sick.

_____ 3. People who make personal phone calls at work.

_____ 4. People who eat lunch at their desks.

_____ 5. People who come to work dressed casually.

_____ 6. People who refuse to participate.

_____ 7. People who don't listen very well.

_____ 8. People who refuse to keep up with technology.

_____ 9. People who gossip.

_____ 10. People who waste time.

_____ 11. People who are arrogant.

_____ 12. People who are rude.

_____ 13. People who can't follow directions.

_____ 14. People who are not willing to learn.

_____ 15. People who don't keep up with current events.

_____ 16. People who have messy desks.

_____ 17. People who are poor spellers.

_____ 18. People who lack ambition.

_____ 19. People who lack energy.

_____ 20. People who act impulsively.

_____ 21. People who keep stuffed animals in their offices.

_____ 22. People who don't have a sense of humor.

_____ 23. People who don't feel passionately about anything.

_____ 24. People who are not organized.

_____ 25. People who don't think logically.

_____ 26. People who are not creative.

Total number of checkmarks: _____

Interpretation

Sometimes we can determine what we are seeking by identifying what we are *not* looking for. Most people check about ten items. Significantly fewer checkmarks suggest that you have an easygoing style of management and that when you influence, you do not do so with "hard sell" tactics. More than fifteen checkmarks may mean you are overly concerned with things you can do little about and consequently may be creating unnecessary stress for yourself. If this is true of you, concentrate your influence efforts on things that really matter and things you can do something about.

Of course, what you want in employees and what you get are two different factors. However, making your staff aware of what you value increases the likelihood that some at least will try to give you what you want. And being aware of what annoys you can help you reduce stress—if you are willing to avoid sweating the "small stuff."

VALUES EMPLOYEES SEE AND SEEK

What employees see

As noted earlier, you cannot *not* communicate. In your every action, in your every word, others will find messages that are intended to be sent, but also messages being inadvertently sent. The secretary who states on her resume, "I am a rabid typist," is signalling that she may be rapid but not very accurate. A single letter could in fact cost her the job.

Employees, like children, notice everything. From the smallest, most casual gesture to the most critical decisions, interpretations are being made about your trustworthiness, your honesty, your value as a manager. The ancient Buddhist admonition, "Anything you do is everything you do," affirms the need for managers to be ever vigilant. Work to align the values you say you believe in with the values you actively promote and protect.

To illustrate, when you ask a question such as, "What lights your fire?" you are doing more than gaining vital information about the preferences and dislikes of staff or team members. You are also demonstrating a sincere concern for your employees as individuals.

155

What employees seek

Before working on the following exercise, make a copy of it. If possible, make a copy for each staff member. Then proceed to rank order the following ten items. You will be ranking them (1 = most important; 10 = least important) according to their importance as motivators for the average employee, in your opinion.

A. _____ Being given responsibility

B. _____ Better pay

C. _____ Opportunity to grow

D. _____ Longer vacations

E. _____ Challenging work

F. _____ Freedom to work without being micromanaged

G. _____ Regular feedback

H. _____ Knowing what I do counts

I. _____ Recognition of my work

J. _____ Chance to participate in decisions

K. _____ Other:

After your employees have had an opportunity to rank order the items in the same way (1 = most important), compare their responses to your own. Chances are, you will be surprised at some of the answers. But you can use this surprise to your advantage: Knowing who values what, you can be much more effective as an influencer.

EXERTING INFLUENCE ON TEAMS

As we've noted several times before, managing is a combination of sustaining the status quo and leading change. As a leader of your team of staff members, you are in a unique position to elicit the best they have to offer. In the words of author Max DePree, "When we think about leaders and the variety of gifts people bring to corporations and institutions, we see that the art of leadership lies in polishing and liberating and enabling those gifts."

When team members feel valued and when values are shared, Win/Win/Win results can be realized. In order to liberate the gifts DePree speaks of, leaders must exert a positive influence on the team and on the environment. Handled responsibly, the task will be easy to execute: you need only view yourself as an enabler, as a polisher of the raw talents lying beneath surfaces. But if you are not demonstrating that you value these talents, then the task will be formidable.

The following lists reflect roles played by two kinds of managers: the enabling leader and the disabling autocrat.

Enabling Behaviors	Disabling Behaviors
Polishes talents	Belittles talents
Welcomes ideas	Dismisses ideas
Empowers	Orders
Listens	Makes snap judgments
Develops self-confidence	Intimidates
Shares credit	Takes credit
Expresses appreciation	Lacks concern for others' feelings
Encourages growth	Attacks mistakes and the mistake-maker

Management expert Tom Peters feels "imagination is the only source of real value in the new economy." As thought leader and team leader you have a unique obligation on your shoulders: to develop the creative talents of your staff members. Before exploring how to influence them to develop and contribute innovative ideas, you can take a quick test of your own creative talents.

Measuring your creativity quotient

Creativity is a vague concept. Many people have tried to define it. In short, creativity boils down to the ability to see what isn't there or to look at what everyone else is looking at but to see what no one else sees. Visionaries have this ability. So do leaders.

As a warm-up, list as many uses as possible for an ordinary pipe-cleaner. Try to list five within one minute. (It may help to have someone quietly announce when the minute has passed so you do not have to keep looking at the clock.)

1. _____

2. _____

3. _____

4. _____

5. _____

Now you're ready for the actual test, which will only take five minutes—one minute per object shown. Do not skip around, but rather spend one minute on each object, in the order presented here. Keep your answers short. The task again is to list as many possible uses for the object displayed beyond the obvious use for which it may have been intended. (Have someone else watch the clock for you if possible.)

1.
1. _____
2. _____
3. _____
4. _____
5. _____

2.
1. _____
2. _____
3. _____
4. _____
5. _____

3.
1. _____
2. _____
3. _____
4. _____
5. _____

4.
1. _____
2. _____
3. _____
4. _____
5. _____

5.

1. _____
2. _____
3. _____
4. _____
5. _____

Total number of ideas: _____

Interpretation

If you were able to generate eighteen ideas in five minutes, you would be among those in the 99th percentile as far as creativity is concerned. Nine ideas would make you about average. If you truly wish to develop your imagination—a quality Einstein regarded as more important than knowledge—prepare similar tests on your own.

Developing your staff's potential

Trust the Collective Capacity to Create—Allow time for ideas to percolate. Provide the necessary resources. Eliminate the fears associated with new ventures. You can do all of this to demonstrate your trust in your team's innovative abilities. You can also express your confidence from time to time, assuring them of your belief that solutions can be found and goals can be met. Applaud past successes and develop a sense of excitement about removing obstacles.

Tolerate Ambiguity—Many organizations exist in cultures of chaos. (So do many employees, judging by the look of their desks.) In some places, that sense of urgency, excitement, unbridled enthusiasm for the new and different is deliberately fostered. While you may not want to go to such extremes with your own staff, you can help them accommodate change by lessening the stress associated with ambiguity. For example, let them know you don't expect an immediate answer to every single question you ask.

Show them, in turn, that you can suspend judgment long enough to refrain from interrupting, that you can listen without making an immediate decision, that you can let ideas incubate when they deserve additional time.

Demonstrate a Willingness to Risk—As Muhammad Ali poetically noted, "The man who has no imagination has no wings." When we soar, we know there is a possibility we will crash to earth. But we also know the exhilaration of flying makes the risk worth taking. Influence your team toward intellectual risk-taking by providing safeguards, by ensuring that caution accompanies risk, but also by rewarding the daring. Show your own willingness to move beyond the ordinary to the extraordinary and recognize others for doing the same.

Make It Known We Can Learn from Mistakes—Disney head Michael Eisner had this to say: "At Disney, we feel the only way to succeed creatively is to fail. Failure is not only tolerated, but fear of criticism for foolish ideas is abolished." It is clear that some executives, at least, understand that missteps always precede the leaps defined as breakthroughs. Here's another CEO echoing the same thought, Microsoft's Bill Gates: "In the corporate world, when someone makes a mistake, everyone runs for cover. At Microsoft, I try to put an end to that kind of thinking."

Think of one specific thing you have done in the last two months to validate effort—whether or not that effort had a

161

successful conclusion. If you can't think of anything, let the absence of specifics influence you to take action—action that will assure your team that you are interested in finding solutions, not finding fault or laying blame. If you were able to isolate a specific action, commit to exhibiting another such action within the next two months.

Celebrate Diversity, Including Diversity of Thought—**Research** confirms that teams composed of members with differences succeed where teams of "clones" fail. In addition to optimizing the diversity that comes from gender, age, race, or culture, you can and should optimize the diversity that comes from differing perspectives.

If you think about it, you will soon realize that thinking that was once on the outer fringe of acceptability often becomes institutionalized in very little time. At least consider, if not welcome, atypical ways of thinking. But realize the transition between welcoming them to your quarters and making them permanent residents there can be a difficult process. To quote Max DePree: "Anything truly creative results in change, and if there is one thing a well-run bureaucracy or institution or major corporation finds difficult to handle, it is change."

PREVIEW

The final chapter takes a look at the long-term outcomes associated with ethical influence. It also tackles the often-maligned practice of self-promotion, which is actually integral to the practice of effective influence. The entrepreneurial spirit and its relationship to principled persuasion is the final topic to be studied.

10 VISION & VISIBILITY

A great many great thinkers have acknowledged the importance of constancy to purpose. Purpose is simply the vision you have for an improvement over existing circumstances. If your vision is not clear or if it is not aligned with the organizational vision, you could be doing irreparable harm to your own career.

As Manchester Consulting reported ("Why Do Newly Promoted Managers Fail?" *Recruiting and Retaining*, sample issue, page 4), the primary reason for failure among newly promoted managers is the inability to work well with others. The second reason is a lack of understanding about expectations between new managers and their own managers.

LONG-TERM OUTCOMES

Strategic plans are used to shape long-term outcomes. They are the stuff by which organizational dreams become reality. But such plans can also be employed on a less-grand scale by divisions, departments, and even individuals. Futurist John Naisbitt advises, though, that "strategic plans are worthless unless there is first strategic vision."

To some, the phrase "strategic planning" is an intimidating one, for many managers think of themselves as people who control and direct and supervise, but not as people who strategize. But when the strategizing process is broken down, it affords managers the opportunity to control and direct the operational events that will lead to long-term outcomes.

1. First, ask questions

The more opinions you can gather, using these (and other) questions as prompts, the more material you will have to build the framework within which critical decisions can be made. Stimulate thinking about present realities in order to influence future results. Once you've codified this information into a strategic plan, you can use it to persuade others to your way of thinking.

- What mistakes have been made recently by those in our same industry?

- What customer complaints could lead to innovative products/ services?

- What substantive issues face us today?

- What will face us tomorrow?

- What are we doing and doing well?

- What are we doing and not doing well?

- What wheels have already been invented?

- How has technology brought about change in the way we do business?

- How might technology bring about change in the way we will conduct business in the future?

- What resources are we wasting by defending the past?

■ What do we need to enhance?

■ How much credence are we willing to place in the prediction by author Warren Bennis: "The factory of the future will have only two employees: a man and a dog. The man will be there to feed the dog. The dog will be there to keep the man from touching the equipment"?

■ What philosophy has transcended the years since our organization was started?

■ How would we define our existing culture?

■ What might our culture become?

■ What measurements will tell us how well we are doing?

■ What should be eliminated?

■ What are we doing for the community/world of which we are part?

■ What are our values?

■ What are our priorities?

■ What makes us unique?

■ Do we have morale problems?

■ Has our ethical stance been clearly defined?

■ Are we thinking globally and acting locally?

■ Are we thinking globally and acting globally?

■ What are we *not* doing that we should be doing?

■ What kind of training will we need to plan for?

■ Have we imagined every possible negative eventuality?

■ Do we have plans in place for dealing with them?

- What combinations might spell improvement or greater profits?

- What potential profit areas are we overlooking?

- What are we doing to encourage creativity?

- What uniqueness will we need in the future?

- What can we do to shape that outcome?

- What demands are customers likely to make?

- What opportunities are we missing?

- What myths surround our efforts?

- What are the realities?

- What basic principles can we agree upon?

- How can we expand our markets?

- What risks are worth taking?

- By what standards do we wish to be known?

- What demands might employees make?

- How can we involve them more?

- What virtual realities should we be helping to create?

- Does mission drive us?

- What is our existing vision?

- To what extent are employees aware of it?

- How familiar are customers and suppliers with our vision?

- How can we improve the way our vision and strategic plans are communicated to those who matter most to us?

- What barriers prevent optimization?

166

- How much/what are we willing to commit?

- What safety issues should concern us?

- What is the ideal workplace?

- Who is the ideal leader?

- What is the ideal company?

- What constitutes excellence in the ideal product or service?

- Who is the ideal employee?

- What messages are we sending?

- What messages should we be sending?

- What distinctions are beginning to blur?

- What will we compete for in the future?

- What market trends should we be paying attention to?

- What is our competitive edge?

- What gaps need to be filled?

2. Next, explore external events that can impact the vision

One of the most valuable and yet most frequently overlooked elements in your planning may be the daily news—and not just the news coming from Wall Street. Whenever an event shatters walls we have erected around traditional thinking, it is time for leaders to review existing policies and make provisions for future eventualities. When crises arise, the need for such review assumes a critical importance. The Oklahoma City bombing, for example, should have made every organizational leader ask, "Can it happen here? If so, are we prepared?" Such scrutiny invariably leads to basic planning: "Do we need an evacuation plan?" "Do we need to review it with employees?"

Of course, there is a balance between learning from crises and responding with knee-jerk measures. Prussian military strategist Karl von Clausewitz warned of transient events, especially those that are brilliant. The glare surrounding them can prevent us from seeing clearly, not only for the present but into the future as well.

As you present your vision and persuade others to adopt it, acknowledge that the title "manager" has not conferred omniscience upon you. Forewarn your followers that you have done the best you could but that you have no crystal ball. Advise that the plan may need adaptation as events unfold. This is where your flexibility comes in. This is also where their willingness to be "defrosted" comes in as well.

Forewarn them, too, that resources are limited and so choices must be made. The delineation of the vision provides an overarching frame for using resources wisely. If safety is indeed part of the vision, then decisions and plans will be made to ensure it. If profits are the overriding concern, then efforts are clustered around that focus. If co-evolution ("the development of new markets via collaboration among competitors, customers, and vendors") appears to be the most promising direction in which to head, then initiatives are begun to attain such unity. If technology seems to offer the best hope for the future, then we plan accordingly. (The fact that over one million cars were sold through the Internet last year alone should serve notice to sales and marketing departments throughout the nation.)

3. Articulate the vision

Formulating your vision requires idealism, imagination, and courage. Facing the darkness of the unknown, distinguishing the outlines of possibilities, then creating a concrete whole out of barely visible shapes is not a job for the faint-of-heart. Once you have that vision, of course, you need to share it with others; you need to persuade them that the future, altered state you are contemplating is worth their time.

They will have to invest more than time, though. They will have to invest the energy required to make mental shifts and then act upon their new ideas. There are those who see what they want to see and those who create what they want to see. Visionaries and their influencees fall into the second category.

4. Then develop plans based on the vision

At some point, you have to move from visionary, concepts-based, strategic planning to operational planning. Such planning represents the practical, logistically based "skin" that meshes with the support system in place for the vision. Less glamorous than the vision, more functional than mere procedures, operational planning examines the incremental steps that eventually lead to the meeting of the visionary goal. Operational planning focuses on routine decisions that face us day by day, quarter by quarter, and even year by year.

Measurable objectives are part of that plan, as are the actions to be taken in prioritized order. The plan anticipates problems and specifies how they will be solved. It is what we arrive at after several contractions and expansions of the original steps: The examination of questions and external events led to narrowed categories, which led to the even more narrowly stated vision. The vision was then expanded via strategic decisions regarding the steps necessary to accomplish the aim of the vision. The steps are then opened wide once more to include the many details that will lead to procedural plans.

To achieve the greatest effectiveness, operational planning must be easily understood by employees at any and all levels of the organization. Directions must be clear and concise. The reporting vehicles must be carefully and fully depicted. Problems that arise as the operations are executed are solved at the lowest possible level. This may be the individual worker or the team assigned to a project. If decisions cannot be reached here, the problem is turned over to first-line supervision. If the problem to be solved or decision to be made is of sufficient magnitude to involve middle management, it is turned over to that level. But always, those closest to the process are the first (and ideally last) to become involved, thus freeing senior management to engage in the activities for which they were hired.

When operational issues are ignored, vision remains in the realm of potential. When long-term strategy is ignored, future growth becomes a haphazard possibility rather than a planned-for objective, pursued with determination along a deliberate course of action.

5. Finally, implement the plan, communicating it as often as possible

If you fail to plan for implementation of your strategy, you will be nullifying the plan itself and the derivative benefits that might have been realized. Effective leaders know they must communicate the spirit and the letter of the new "law" that will govern individual and departmental behaviors in the years ahead. Repeatedly.

The manager who makes strategic plans, either for a simple work unit or for the corporate body itself, has to define the relationship between her scope of control and the big picture. Change is integral to such planning. Without it, the manager is simply maintaining and not growing.

The change that accompanies growth led Graham Briggs, vice president of Charles River Data Systems, to regard the very thought of strategic planning as "damn scary." He acknowledges that it's easier to simply declare, "Next year's going to be better" and leave it at that. Of course, improvement comes from more than just wishful thinking. It comes from planning, very careful planning.

Your staff will have to stretch to meet the demands of your vision. As they do so, new opportunities will open up. If you manage your staff without a vision, they will remain deaf to the knock of opportunity. They will remain unattuned to possibilities and unaware of the potential impact of external events, events with long-term implications. In the words of master strategist Peter Drucker, "Long-range planning does not deal with future decisions, but with the future of present decisions."

SELF-PROMOTION

Promoting your vision means promoting yourself—directly and indirectly. While the intent of your promotion may not be self-promotion, the fact remains that taking a persuasive stance increases your visibility.

Actions are couched in braided threads. You may not intend to self-promote, but it is a factor. What you do can seldom be viewed in terms of stark black-or-white factors alone. Typically, there will be multiple reasons that explain why that action was taken, and multiple consequences that will evolve from that action.

Yes, there will be greater attention paid to you in the course of proposing, developing, and implementing your idea. But to equate idea promotion with self-promotion entirely would be wrong. Know that more people will recognize you if you embark upon a persuasion journey. Know, too, that if your persuasions are not fair, ethical, dignified, and respectful, you may soon find the attention paid to you being transformed into apathy or perhaps even active dislike. Principled persuasion is a career booster. Unprincipled persuasion is a career *breaker*.

Throughout this book, you have been encouraged to keep an open mind about the meaning of certain words. *Power*, for example, is often associated with abuse. Dr. Tom Rusk, however, defines power as "creative influence." Don't be overly concerned with words. Do be excessively concerned with the purpose behind the words you use. If you are not seeking Win/Win/Win outcomes; if you are focusing on self-aggrandizement rather than self-growth; if you are thinking only of how you can get ahead rather than how others can advance; then you may be persuading but you are not persuading on principle.

Research by David McClelland of Harvard reveals that different people are motivated by different forces to do their very best work. To illustrate, which of the possible interpretations listed below is closest to the way you would identify the man in the suit?

a. This man is probably an entertainer who makes his living by singing or performing.

b. This man could easily be a manager who has organized an elaborate going-away party for a much respected retiring employee.

c. This man may well be someone who volunteers time on the weekend to work with children in hospitals or with the elderly in nursing homes.

While there is no right or wrong answer to this kind of mental perception test, the answers do indicate the kind of position that most motivates individuals to do their best work. If you chose answer (a), you are likely to be a person who is most driven by the need for achievement. This sort of person is an entrepreneur at heart, a self-starter, a person who sets her own goals.

Selecting answer (b) reveals a need for power. Before you recoil, note that McClelland's research found that the best managers showed a strong need for power. They seek accomplishment via organizing and directing the work of others.

Answer (c) reflects a true concern for other people. This sort of person has a strong need for affiliation and is best suited for work that helps people such as customer service or social work.

THE ENTREPRENEURIAL SPIRIT

While one particular drive predominates, each of us possesses a combination of achievement, power, and affiliation drives. When you choose to translate your vision from the realm of possibility to the realm of actuality, you are exercising your achievement drive and then your power drive. The two work in concert to help you reach your goal. And if you remember to celebrate successes, to share credit, to thank your staff, to manage in a participative fashion, then you are employing affiliative techniques as well on your way to achievement.

The vision begins with your excitement about a better way of doing things—better for you, better for others, better for the organization itself. And when you help create positive change for multiple beneficiaries, then you have exemplified principled persuasion. More power to you and to your ideas.

SUGGESTED READING

Alexrod, Alan, and Jim Holtje, *201 Ways to Say No Gracefully and Effectively* (New York: McGraw-Hill), 1997.

Augustine, Norman, *Augustine's Travels* (New York: AMACOM), 1998.

Benun, Ilise, editor, *The Art of Self Promotion* (P.O. Box 23, Hoboken, NJ 07030).

Bick, Julie, *All I Really Need to Know about Businesss I Learned at Microsoft* (New York: Simon & Schuster Pocketbooks), 1997.

Blanchard, Ken, *Gung Ho!* (New York: William Morrow), 1998.

Burris, Daniel, *Technotrends* (New York: HarperCollins), 1993.

Caroselli, Marlene, *The Language of Leadership* (Amherst, MA: HRD Press), 1990.

Cohen, Herb, *You Can Negotiate Anything* (Secaucus, NJ: L. Stuart Publishers), 1980.

DiZazzo, Raymond, *Saying the Right Thing: The 4 Secrets of Powerful Communications* (Naperville, IL: Sourcebooks, Inc.), 1997.

Driscoll, Dawn-Marie, W. Michael Hoffman, and Edward S. Petry, *The Ethical Edge: Tales of Organizations That Have Faced Moral Crises* (Portland, OR: Master Media Ltd.), 1997.

Fisher, Roger, and William Ury, *Getting to Yes* (Boston: Houghton Mifflin), 1981.

Giacalone, Robert, and Jerald Greenberg, *AntiSocial Behavior in Organizations* (Thousand Oaks, CA: Sage Publications), 1996.

Goleman, Daniel, *Emotional Intelligence* (New York: Bantam Books), 1995.

Handy, Charles, *The Gods of Management* (New York: Oxford University Press), 1995.

Hurt, Floyd, *Rousing Creativity* (Charlottesville, VA: Probe Press, Inc.), 1996.

Jackson, Tim, *Inside Intel* (New York: Dutton), 1997.

Jandt, Fred, and Paul Gillette, *Win-Win Negotiating* (New York: Wiley & Sons), 1985.

Kayser, Thomas, *Mining Group Gold* (New York: Publishers Group), 1995.

Macchiavelli, Niccolo, *The Prince* (New York: Everyman's Library), 1958.

Mackay, Harvey, *Dig Your Well Before You're Thirsty* (New York, Doubleday), 1996.

Nierenberg, Gerard, *Negotiating the Big Sale* (Homewood, IL: Business One Irwin), 1992.

Pinchot, Gifford, *Intrapreneuring* (New York: Harper and Row), 1985.

Price Waterhouse Change Integration® Team, *The Paradox Principles* (Chicago: Irwin Professional Publishing), 1996.

Rusk, Tom, *The Power of Ethical Persuasion* (New York: The Penguin Group), 1993.

Sheehy, Barry, *Winning the Race for Value* (New York: AMACOM Books), 1996.

Slater, Robert, *Get Better or Get Beaten!* (Chicago: Irwin Professional Publishing), 1994.

Spence, Gerry, *How to Argue and Win Every Time* (New York: St. Martin's Press), 1996.

ABOUT THE AUTHOR

Dr. Marlene Caroselli is the author of three dozen business books, listed at the Amazon.com Web site. The first of those books, *The Language of Leadership*, was published by HRD Press and was chosen by Newbridge's Executive Book Club as a main selection. The most recent, *Principled Persuasion*, also available from HRD Press, was recently named a Director's Choice by Doubleday Book Club.

In addition to books, Dr. Caroselli writes for several online magazines and for Stephen Covey's *Excellence* publications, as well as for the *National Business Employment Weekly* and Dartnell's *Motivated to Sell* newsletter. When she is not writing, Dr. Caroselli conducts corporate training and delivers keynote addresses for such organizations as the U.S. Navy, the Institute for International Research, the State of Michigan, the U.S. Department of the Interior, the Public Relations Society of America, and Xerox Corporation. She has also served as an adjunct professor at UCLA and National University.

You can reach Dr. Caroselli at 716-227-6512 (fax: 716-227-6191) or by e-mail: mccpd@aol.com to ask about workshops, presentations, or related topics. Write her at:

Center for Professional Development
324 Latona Road, Suite 1600
Rochester, New York 14626-2714
or visit http://hometown.aol.com/mccpd.

INDEX